STUDENT PROJECTS

An Introduction to Research and Communication Skills

Hugh Robertson
Cartoons by Cuyler Black

PIPERHILL

Student Projects
An Introduction to Research and Communication Skills

Third edition

Piperhill Publications, Ottawa.
www.piperhill.ca

ISBN 0-9693068-8-1

Printed and bound in Canada.

National Library of Canada Cataloguing in Publication
Robertson, Hugh, 1939-
Student projects: an introduction to research and communication skills
Cartoons by Cuyler Black
3rd edition.

Originally published under title: The project book.
Includes bibliographical references.
For grades 8–11.
ISBN 0-9693068-8-1

        1. Report writing. I. Black, Cuyler II. Title.

LB1047.3.R63 2002   808'.02   C2002-904994-6

Cover and Interior Design: Avante Graphics and Sharper Images

This book was manufactured in Canada using acid-free and recycled paper.

Contents

Acknowledgements

Student Projects is the outcome of many years of teaching. Therefore, it is really a joint venture involving numerous students who have shared in developing and refining the procedures and practices described in the manual. To all these students who made every day a learning experience for me, I offer my grateful appreciation. In particular, I am indebted to Aaron Barth, Joey Brothers, Sarah Dudley, Matt Labarge, Olivia McNee, and Darren Prevost for providing the sample assignments.

Four talented teachers have played a special role in shaping *Student Projects*. Their expertise and experience, ideas and insights have enhanced this book immeasurably. My sincerest thanks to Elizabeth Campbell, Nancy Jowett, Hugh Penton, and Marilynne Sinclair for their perceptive comments and practical suggestions, as well as their patience and support.

Dedicated to the memories of
John Connelly, Joseph Mouaikel,
and Sami Qirbi.

Introduction

Every research project or essay is a journey of exploration and discovery into unknown territory. Just as an explorer setting off on an expedition needs to pack provisions, a route map, and equipment, such as a compass and a Global Positioning System, you also need to be prepared when you embark on your assignments.

This guide will provide you with both the essentials for your backpack — the important research and communication skills — as well as a sense of direction for your "expedition." The guide will introduce you to a variety of techniques, from the more traditional practices to the latest technological methods. Equip yourself with both, for although a GPS can determine locations precisely, batteries can fail and a backup compass will prevent you from ending up in an alligator swamp.

Start your journey with the research report (pages 3–22) because it introduces the basic research and communication skills. Master these basic skills and you can then launch yourself on any of the other expeditions — from research papers to public speaking. You can always consult the "route map" on the next page if you ever lose your way.

The route map outlines a basic pathway that underlies all the different types of expeditions. There are minor detours on the pathway depending on the nature of your expedition — for example, whether you are writing an essay based on a single primary text or on multiple secondary sources. The pathway or process is flexible; use it, experiment with it, and reshape it to suit your needs. Armed with a command of the skills and the process, you will be able to handle all your assignments with speed, confidence, and success.

THE RESEARCH AND WRITING PROCESS

Preparation / Research

```
┌─────────────────────────────┐
│            Topic            │
└─────────────────────────────┘
              │
              ▼
┌─────────────────────────────┐
│            Focus            │
└─────────────────────────────┘
              │
              ▼
┌─────────────────────────────┐
│      Search for Sources     │
└─────────────────────────────┘
              │
              ▼
┌─────────────────────────────┐
│       Purpose / Question    │
└─────────────────────────────┘
              │
              ▼
┌─────────────────────────────┐
│      Preparatory Reading    │
└─────────────────────────────┘
              │
              ▼
┌──────────────┐
│   Working    │
│   Outline    │
└──────────────┘
              │
              ▼
┌─────────────────────────────┐
│       Assemble Sources      │
└─────────────────────────────┘
              │
              ▼
┌─────────────────────────────┐
│      Record Information      │
└─────────────────────────────┘
```

Presentation / Writing

```
┌─────────────────────────────┐
│      Shape the Outlines      │
│        Basic Outline         │
│       Skeleton Outline       │
│      Point-form Outline      │
└─────────────────────────────┘
              │
              ▼
┌─────────────────────────────┐
│         Rough Draft          │
│         Title Page           │
│          Contents            │
│        Introduction          │
│            Body              │
│         Conclusion           │
│          Appendix            │
│        Documentation         │
└─────────────────────────────┘
              │
              ▼
┌─────────────────────────────┐
│            Revise            │
└─────────────────────────────┘
              │
              ▼
┌─────────────────────────────┐
│             Edit             │
└─────────────────────────────┘
              │
              ▼
┌─────────────────────────────┐
│           Proofread          │
└─────────────────────────────┘
              │
              ▼
┌─────────────────────────────┐
│          Final Copy          │
└─────────────────────────────┘
```

2 The Research Report

Reports usually explain or describe something. For example, a geography report might explain weather patterns in the Rocky Mountains, while a history report might trace the course of the War of 1812. Reports are often biographical, such as detailing the life of an author. In an English class you might also be asked to describe conditions in Chekhov's Russia or to explain a literary technique, such as dramatic monologue. You will be required to produce explanatory reports, usually based on research, in most of your subjects.

A report provides factual information to help explain and clarify something, but it does not present an argument or a point of view. In other words, **a report has a theme,** but, unlike an essay, it does not have a thesis or an opinion.

RESEARCH

Selecting the Topic

Occasionally you may have the freedom to select your own topic for a research report. In most cases, however, your teacher will decide on a topic, or alternatively, provide a list of topics from which you can choose. For example, your geography teacher may decide on the Great Lakes as a topic for a research report. We will use this topic as our example to illustrate the process for researching and presenting a report. If you have to prepare a report in another subject, such as English or history, simply follow the same process.

In our example, the teacher has assigned a short report of 800 – 900 words on any aspect of the Great Lakes. Although the teacher has set the topic, it will be your responsibility to narrow the topic and to choose an aspect of the Great Lakes to investigate, and then to formulate your own research question.

Before starting any projects, you need to understand the **specific requirements for each project.** Get answers to the following questions from your teachers before you start. Both the questions and the answers form an important stage in preparing for your expedition.

- How many sources should be used?

- What types of sources should be used?

- How long should the project be?

- When is it due? Are there late penalties?

- Are stages, such as research notes and drafts, due at specific times?

- Will there be class time to work on the project?

- Will an oral presentation also be required?

- How will it be marked? For example, will the research as well as the final report be marked?

- Is a sample marking form available?

- Should you use illustrations?

- How should the completed report be structured? For example, what should you include in the introduction and the conclusion?

- Should sections be identified by subheadings?

- How should the sources be acknowledged and listed?

- Should a written report be typed or handwritten?

Once you know when the project is due, **start planning a schedule** for the different stages so that it is comfortably completed before the deadline. Not only will you be developing important time-management skills but you will also avoid an inferior project hastily put together at the last minute.

Narrowing the Focus

The Great Lakes is too broad and general a topic to explore for a short research project. Your final report would either be much too long or it would be too superficial. Narrowing the topic to a specific feature or aspect of the Great Lakes is an important first step.

The best way to narrow a broad topic is to read and think about it. Textbooks and encyclopedias are useful for the exploratory reading and thinking.[1] You may also find films and videos on your topic. As you read and view videos, try to isolate **as many features and aspects of your topic** that you think will provide an interesting focus for investigation.

Another way to increase your list of ideas, features, and aspects is to form a group with other students and brainstorm the topic. **Brainstorming** is an exciting process for generating ideas, raising questions, and discovering interesting aspects of a topic.

List all the ideas from your reading, thinking, and brainstorming in a notebook or type them up on a computer, as shown below. A notebook, either paper or electronic, is a good place to list all your ideas and questions for each project. We will call it your *Ideas and Questions Journal — I.Q. Journal* for short.

The Great Lakes	
Birds	Migration
Pollution	Sea birds
Industry	Lampreys
Fishing	Chemical waste
PCBs	Hydro-electricity
Recreation	Dioxins
Welland Canal	Manure
Climate	Sewage
Shipping	Naval battles
Niagara Falls	Shipwrecks
Smuggling	Nuclear energy
Geology	Thermal energy
Glaciation	Coast guard
Cargo	Islands
Water levels	Tourism
Zebra mussels	Lighthouses

You can also use diagrammatic techniques, such as "mapping," to brainstorm. One member of the group can use the chalkboard and start with the topic in the centre. Other students can suggest ideas and aspects that can then be broken down further, as shown opposite. Alternatively, the teacher can lead the brainstorming with the whole class suggesting ideas. Brainstorming is a great way to get the creative juices flowing.

Write down as many ideas as you can in your *I.Q. Journal*, regardless of whether they are major features or minor aspects. The longer the list, the better your chances are of finding one that appeals to you. Next, draw up a short list of those features that interest you, and then **choose one** on which to focus your research.

After carefully considering your list of features, you decide to focus on "pollution" because of your concern about its impact on the Great Lakes. It is a good idea to have one or two backup features listed in your *I.Q. Journal*, in case you run into difficulties with your first choice. For example, you may jot down "Shipwrecks" and "Glaciation" as backup alternatives.

Usually the narrowing process will involve a number of stages and it may also require some more exploratory reading and brainstorming. For example, a short project on pollution in the Great Lakes would produce a broad and superficial report. After further reading, you discover that there are different forms of pollution, such as biological, chemical, and bacterial. You might decide to focus on biological pollution and then narrow it further to the zebra mussel invasion of the Great Lakes.

Isolating the zebra mussel problem places a spotlight on it like a singer on a stage. Clearly illuminated like a solo singer in a bright shaft of light on a dark stage, the zebra mussel problem is now the **sole focus** of your attention.

Select a feature that you can handle comfortably. While pollution might be too broad for a short project, a feature that is too small is also not suitable. For example, narrowing "Birds" to a single species, such as the jaeger, would be too difficult unless you are an expert bird watcher. Think carefully before you choose. Discuss your choice with your classmates and with your teacher, and then ensure that your teacher approves your decision.

Narrowing the topic is an important stage in the process of preparing your report because the **feature or aspect that you select will provide the focus for your research.** The analogy of the ice cream cone opposite clearly illustrates the narrowing or focusing process.

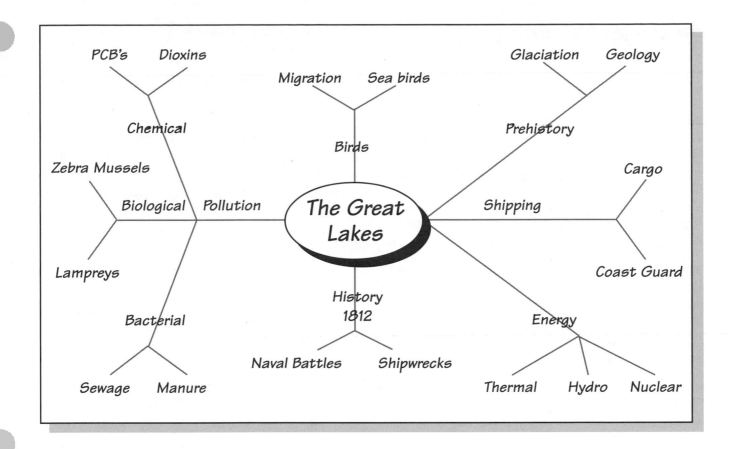

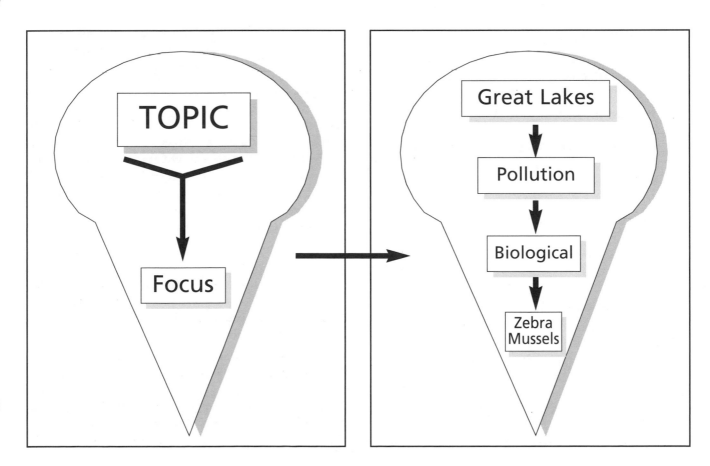

Searching for Sources

Once you have narrowed your topic to a specific focus, your next step is to start compiling a list of sources of information. If there are not enough sources on your first choice, you will have to substitute your second choice. It is important to determine as soon as possible whether there is sufficient information available before you continue.

There is an array of searching techniques and tools to find sources of information on almost every imaginable topic. Some searching tools are in print form, while others are electronic (or digital). Electronic material is either available online through the Internet or on CD-ROM or DVD. Learn to use **both print and electronic searching techniques** because, although some tools, such as indexes are usually produced in electronic form today, the earlier volumes are often only available in print.

We have listed below a selection of the techniques and tools, with examples, available to you. Space does not permit a detailed explanation of how to use them. However, advice is available from librarians and most computer search engines also have help sections on searching procedures. But remember that hands-on personal practice is always the best teacher. Do not attempt to use all these techniques immediately; rather try them out gradually as you undertake your research projects.

- The **catalogue** lists most of the resources held in a library and, therefore, it is usually the best place to start your research.

- **Periodical indexes** are helpful research tools because they enable you to locate articles in hundreds of magazines and journals. The following are especially useful for research projects: *Canadian Periodical Index* and *Readers' Guide to Periodical Literature*.

- **Newspaper indexes** provide quick access to newspaper articles. Some indexes include a number of newspapers, such as the *Canadian NewsDisc*, while others cover just one newspaper, such as *The New York Times Index*.

- **Biographical indexes,** such as the *Biography Index* and *Contemporary Authors,* are especially useful if you are studying a person.

- **Bibliographies** list books, articles, and other sources on specific topics. They are helpful because someone else has done the searching for you. Examples of bibliographies are: *Bibliographia Canadiana* and *Women in American History.*

- **Browsing** in the library is an effective way of expanding your list of sources. Locate your "browsing area" by using the catalogue to determine which shelves hold books on your topic. Then check the table of contents and indexes in books relevant to your topic.

- The **reference shelves,** containing encyclopedias, atlases, and yearbooks, can be a profitable area for browsing.

- There is a wide range of **non-print material** available in the form of maps, statistics, photographs, taped interviews, films, videos, television and radio clips, and computer programs. Indexes and directories are available that will help you track down this material for your projects.

- Talk to your **teachers and librarians.** They will be able to provide you with useful leads for sources.

- There are often **experts in your community** whom you might interview for your projects.

- You can also contact experts by **email** or raise questions through **discussion groups** on the Internet.

- Compile a list of **resources in your community,** such as museums, art galleries, libraries, archives, and historical societies.

As you search, you will be looking only for sources of information on the aspect or feature that you have selected as the focus for your research. Using a variety of sources can improve a project. To increase the variety of your sources, you might set them out on separate pages of notepaper, headed "Books," "Articles," "Internet," "Audio/Visual," and so forth. As you discover sources, list them under the appropriate heading, as shown on the opposite page.

If you are using a computer, you can set up files as "electronic notepaper" in a word processor. Save each of the files with headings, such as "Books," "Articles," "Internet," and "Audio/Visual," as explained above. Then type in the source details in the manner demonstrated on the opposite page.

This list of sources is called your **Working Bibliography.** Make sure you record all the essential details, such as author, title, and publication information because you will need these details for compiling your final bibliography. The procedure for preparing the final bibliography is explained later.

Code	Books
GL	_The Great Lakes: An environmental atlas and resource book._ (1995). Chicago: United States Environmental Protection Agency and Toronto: Environment Canada.

Code	Audio / Visual
DGL	_Discover the Great Lakes: The ecosystem of the Great Lakes-St. Lawrence._ (1997). [CD-ROM]. Ottawa: Environment Canada.

Code	Articles
MM	Zorpette, G. (1996, August). Mussel mayhem. _Scientific American, 275_, 22-23.
LE	Leahy, S. (2001, December 3). Lake Erie's small but toxic killers. _Maclean's, 114_, 16.
FEB	Binder, D. (2000, July 11). Great Lakes face endless battle with marine invaders. _New York Times_, F4.

Code	Internet
ZMP	Ram, J.L. (April, 1997). _The zebra mussel page_. <http://www.science.wayne.edu/~jram/zmussel.htm> (2002, March 20).
EI	_Economic impacts of zebra mussel infestation_. (N.d.). <http://www.wes.army.mil/el/zebra/zmis/...impacts_of_zebra_infestation.htm> (2002, March 10).

Continue listing all your sources, as shown in the examples above. The **code** is a shortened form of the title that will identify the source during the research. For example, MM stands for "Mussel mayhem" and LE represents the key words in the title "Lake Erie's small but toxic killers." There is no need to sign the source material out of the library at this stage. You are just listing the sources and determining **if there is enough potential material available** on the focus of your research.

How many sources should you list in your Working Bibliography? This will depend both on the length of the project and on your teacher's instructions. If the teacher does not specify the number of sources required, try to list up to ten sources for a short report. It is not likely that you will be able to track them all down later and some may not be relevant for the research. But as you will probably only use between four and six sources for the project, you should be safe with an initial list of ten sources.

Once you are satisfied that you have enough sources listed in your Working Bibliography, you are ready to move on to the next stage of the research. Remember that if you are having difficulty discovering relevant sources, you will probably have to change the focus of your project. That is the advantage of having a couple of backup features ready in your _I.Q. Journal_. It is better to change course in the early stages of a project than to discover that you have insufficient sources as the deadline approaches. You can avert crises by careful planning.

It is a good idea to keep your group working together throughout the project. Members of the group can cooperate in developing working bibliographies. If you know the focus of each member's research, you can jot down relevant sources that you may come across in your searching. Sharing in this way can expand each member's source list and help develop cooperative work habits.

Another advantage of developing your Working Bibliography in the early stages of the project is that interesting ideas might emerge that may serve as the purpose of your report. Titles and subtitles of sources often suggest challenging research questions. Jot all these ideas and questions down in your _I.Q. Journal_.

Defining the Purpose

The next step is to define more clearly the direction of your research. In other words, what is the precise purpose or objective of your report? You may already have developed some ideas while you were building your Working Bibliography and then listed them in your *I.Q. Journal*.

It may be necessary to read more about the focus of your project to generate additional ideas about the direction it will take. For example, after further reading, you discover that investigating the impact of the zebra mussels on all the Great Lakes is still too broad. Since you found a number of sources about the zebra mussel problem in Lake Erie, you decide to narrow the focus of your research to Lake Erie. Because the research process is flexible, further narrowing can take place at any stage.

A single, challenging question is the best way to launch your research and to give direction to your project. For example, you may formulate your research question as follows: "How did the zebra mussels invade the Great Lakes?" Alternatively, you may phrase the purpose of your research as a statement: "The purpose of my research is to explain how the zebra mussels invaded the Great Lakes."

Consider the time assigned for the project and its length. Do not get carried away and pose a question that would produce a book. Also do not launch yourself on a journey that might be too difficult. Attempting to demonstrate the impact of zebra mussels on algae growth in Lake Erie might be too complex unless you have a good knowledge of science. On the other hand, do not suggest unimaginative questions, such as "What are zebra mussels?"

Gather your group and brainstorm possible research questions for your project. Remember to write any ideas and questions down in your *I.Q. Journal* or sketch them out in "map" form, as shown below.

Reflect on the possible directions your report might take before deciding on **one.** After talking to your teacher, you decide to phrase your question as follows: "What impact have the zebra mussels had on Lake Erie?" Alternatively, you could state the objective of the report as follows: "The purpose of my research is to describe the impact of the zebra mussels on Lake Erie." Either way, the direction of your project is clearly mapped out.

Avoid posing two questions because you may head off in two separate directions and that could be disastrous at the start of your expedition. With a single research question or statement of purpose you will have set your compass or GPS and established the direction of the project. **Your sole task now is to answer the question** — the answer will be the final destination on your journey.

Once you have established the direction of your report and you know that there are sufficient sources available, you are ready to embark on the next stage of your journey. There is little chance now of getting lost in the woods. We have inserted a route map on the opposite page to guide you.

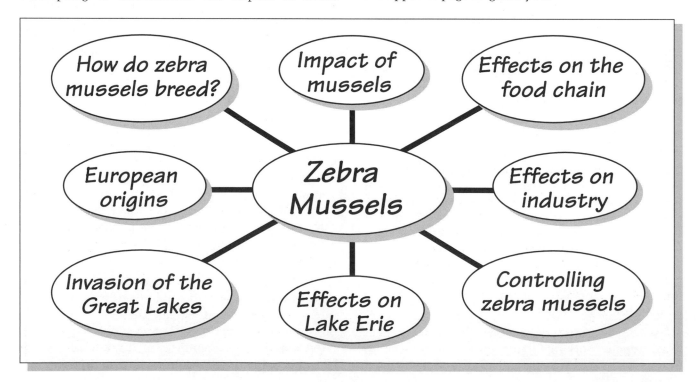

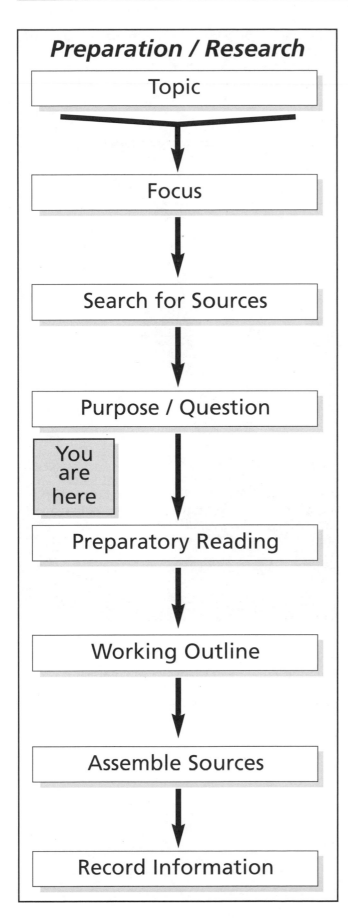

Preparation / Research

Topic

Focus

Search for Sources

Purpose / Question

You are here

Preparatory Reading

Working Outline

Assemble Sources

Record Information

Preparatory Reading

Before starting the detailed research, you need to develop a better understanding of the focus of your report: in our example, the zebra mussel problem in Lake Erie. As with the earlier exploratory reading, textbooks and reference works, such as encyclopedias, are useful for the preparatory reading. You might also locate one or two shorter sources from your Working Bibliography. Pre-reading some of your shorter sources will provide an overview of their content and indicate how useful they might be for the research.

Much of the reading, thinking, brainstorming, and even some of your research notes will not appear in the final copy. But all this "invisible" work provides an essential foundation for your report. A research project is like an iceberg — the ten percent above the water represents your final product. But just as all that ice under the water keeps the iceberg afloat, the "invisible" work prevents your report from disappearing under the water.

The preparatory reading is a crucial part of the underpinnings of the iceberg. It will provide you with the background knowledge that you will need to develop perceptive questions during the research. It will also help you judge what is relevant and reliable in the answers. In addition to learning more about the focus of your research, the preparatory reading also allows you to start shaping the structure of your report.

The Working Outline

Your report will be structured around three main parts: the introduction, the body, and the conclusion. **It is in the body where the answer to your question will be developed.** Set up a separate page in your *I.Q. Journal* headed "Working Outline," as shown below.

Your specific purpose is to investigate and describe the impact of the zebra mussels on Lake Erie. As you undertake the preparatory reading, keep the question or purpose uppermost in your mind. As you read, write down the main factors that you anticipate will help you answer your question. There is no special order at this stage. Just list as many major factors in the body of the Working Outline as possible.

Gather your group to consider the outlines. Make copies of each member's Working Outline and discuss and brainstorm one another's outlines. Getting the perspectives and insights of your peers always generates novel and interesting ideas. Revise and fine tune your Working Outline and then discuss it with your teacher.

Displayed below is a sample outline that might emerge from the preparatory reading in response to our question about the impact of the zebra mussels on Lake Erie.

Working Outline

A. Introduction

B. Body

    I. Water clarity

    II. Aquatic life

    III. Birds

    IV. Fishing

    V. Recreation

    VI. Industry

C. Conclusion

Sometimes the body of your outline may have too many factors or sections. You may have to eliminate or consolidate some sections to reduce the length of the outline. There is no magic number, but from three to six sections in the body will provide a good working structure. What is crucial is that each section, factor, or item in the body of the Working Outline must be **directly linked to the question or purpose** of the research. The research question shapes the body of the Working Outline — the question and the outline are both linked by an indivisible umbilical cord.

The Working Outline is not a final plan for the report. It is a **flexible plan** because you may modify it during the detailed research by eliminating some sections and adding more. But the Working Outline does supply a tentative structure that will help shape your report and provide a framework for the next step, the detailed research.

Pause for a moment to look back at your route:

- The teacher assigned a topic.
- You narrowed the topic to one focal feature.
- You compiled a Working Bibliography.
- You defined the purpose/question.
- You undertook the preparatory reading.
- You developed a Working Outline.

Recording Information

Now you are ready to start the detailed research and record the information you need to answer your question and compose your report. First you have to track down your sources. If you have difficulty locating some of the sources on your list, ask your librarian for assistance. Do not panic if you cannot find all the sources in your Working Bibliography. Not all the sources will be available in your school and community libraries and that is why you listed more than you really needed in your Working Bibliography.

You cannot remember everything you read and, therefore, **you need a method for recording and organizing your information.** It is impossible to develop a good report without an organized collection of research notes.

One of the advantages of having a Working Outline is that it provides a framework for your research notes. Simply write the sections of your Working Outline on separate pages of notepaper, as shown below.

If you are using a computer, you can create "electronic notepaper" by setting up files in your word processor (Microsoft *Word* or Corel *WordPerfect*). Then type the section headings of the Working Outline at the top of each "page," as just described.

Your research system is set up and you are ready to go. Take one of your sources and start reading through looking for information relevant to your research question. For example, if you were using the article "Lake Erie's small but toxic killers" in *Maclean's* magazine, you would discover on page 16 that fish-eating birds are dying in increasing numbers from toxins originating in zebra mussels. You would write the note briefly **in your own words** on the page (or in the file) headed "B. III. Birds" because the information is relevant to the impact of zebra mussels on birds.

You must **indicate the source of each note.** This is easily done by coding your sources, as demonstrated on page 7. For example, using key words from the title, the article was coded "LE" for "Lake Erie's small but toxic killers." In addition to the source, you must also mention the page number for the information. Therefore, "LE 16" indicates that the information is from page 16 of the article "Lake Erie's small but toxic killers," as shown below.

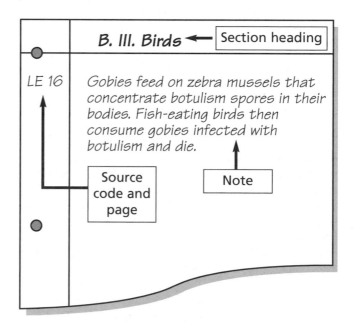

In recording this note, you have:

- Discovered information relevant to your research question.
- Recorded the details under the appropriate section heading.
- Indicated the source and page number.

The whole process of recording the information needed to develop an answer to your research question is covered in the three steps above. **This is the basis of the research process,** whether you are writing your notes by hand or keying them in on a computer.

Continue reading through source LE looking specifically for information on the impact of the zebra mussels on Lake Erie. On the same page as the previous note, a scientist describes gobies infected by zebra mussels as "poison pills" and you decide to write down his exact words as a quotation. Use quotation marks to show that it is a direct quotation from the source, as demonstrated below. The note is entered under "B. III. Birds" because it deals with the loss of fish-eating birds.

B. III. Birds	
LE 16	Gobies feed on zebra mussels that concentrate botulism spores in their bodies. Fish-eating birds then consume gobies infected with botulism and die.
LE 16	"Gobies are becoming little poison pills," claims biologist Jeff Robinson.

Once you have completed your research from source LE, move on to your next source, for example, the Internet article "Economic impacts of zebra mussel infestation," coded EI for "Economic impacts . . ." It is a good idea to bookmark your Internet sources and also to print copies of the shorter articles. In the second paragraph of source EI, you find reference to the impact of zebra mussels on swimming beaches. Because the information concerns swimming which is a recreational activity, you record the information on the page headed "B.V. Recreation," as shown below.

B. V. Recreation	
EI 1	Many beaches are covered with sharp-edged mussel shells and rotting mussel flesh.

On the same page in source EI, you read about the expensive problems zebra mussels are creating for industry by blocking water intake pipes. You record this information under section "B.VI. Industry," as shown in the next column.

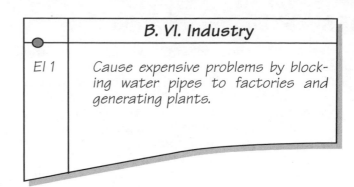

B. VI. Industry	
EI 1	Cause expensive problems by blocking water pipes to factories and generating plants.

And so you continue reading through your sources, searching for information relevant to your research question. Then record it, either on notepaper or on your computer, under the appropriate sections of your Working Outline. Once you fill a hand-written page, continue writing on the reverse side and then start a new page, if necessary. All new pages must be assigned correct headings.

Try to use at least three different sources for your information. If you use only one source, it may be unbalanced, or erroneous, or biased. By relying on at least three different authorities, you get a wider range of views and information. You may also be able to confirm or reject controversial information.

The bulk of your researched information will be recorded under the section headings of the body of your Working Outline. But you should also be aware of the requirements for the introduction and the conclusion so that you may note relevant ideas and information under those headings too. Read the descriptions of the introduction and the conclusion on pages 15 and 18 before you start researching in your sources and recording relevant details.

Since collecting information is such an important stage in preparing your report, you should allow **at least one third of the time** your teacher has assigned to the project for doing the research. Try to collect as much relevant information as possible; it will improve the quality of your report.

Keep these points in mind:

- Write the information in your own words.
- Be concise, clear, and accurate in your notes.
- Keep quotations to a minimum.
- Your notes must be relevant to your research question.
- If a piece of information does not fit under one of the section headings, you either have to create another major section or discard the information as irrelevant.
- Do not create a General or Miscellaneous section.

PRESENTATION

Now that the digging is over, you can start composing your answer to the question — the theme of your report.[2] Projects are like coins: one side is the research, the other is the presentation. Try to present the theme to your readers as clearly as possible. It is largely your writing skills combined with the structure of the report that will determine the clarity of your theme.

Shaping the structure is your first task. The ABC formula (A. Introduction, B. Body, C. Conclusion) on which the Working Outline was based is a simple and effective model for structuring reports and many other types of projects.

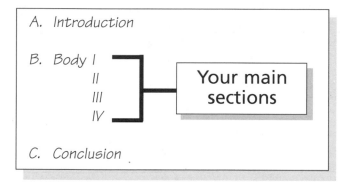

Shaping the Outlines

Once you have finished your research, your notes will be grouped on separate pages according to the sections of your Working Outline. It is impossible to write your final report directly from your notes. A series of outlining and drafting stages will help you produce a much better report.

Basic Outline

This is a major stage in composing your report because you will be establishing the basic structure of the body which is the most important part. Set aside adequate time to read and reread your notes. Since you are planning the structure of the answer and your answer is a direct response to your question, **keep the question constantly in mind** as you study your notes.

You may discover that some sections have too little information, or perhaps contain irrelevant information, and that they will have to be eliminated. Some of the information may actually fit better in another section and will have to be transferred. If you are using a computer, it is easy to transfer notes by cutting and pasting.

It is possible that you may also have to rearrange the order of the main sections of the body as you wrestle with the structure. If you have to eliminate sections or change their order, you will also have to alter the numbers of the sections. It is a simple task to change the numbers of the section headings at the top of the note pages to reflect the new order.

Some sections had to be changed in our example. We discovered that the ability of the zebra mussels to filter lake water (I. Water clarity) best fitted under "II. Aquatic life." So we eliminated "I. Water clarity," transferred some notes, and then changed the numbers of the other sections, although we kept them in the same order.

The diagrams below illustrate the changes and also demonstrate how you convert your Working Outline into the Basic Outline. Once you have established the Basic Outline, the basic structure of your report is in place. Ask yourself if **the structure satisfactorily addresses your research question.**

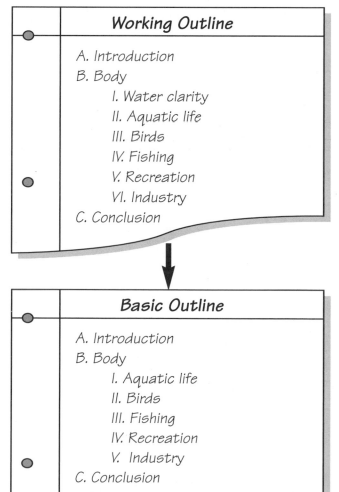

Skeleton Outline

The advantage of having your notes separated on pages according to the structure of your Basic Outline will now become clear. Most of your notes will be contained in the body sections. You may also have jotted down some information and suggestions under the introduction and the conclusion.

The next step is to read through the notes of each section separately, looking for the important details needed to develop and support that section. Because you have a good knowledge of your notes by now, deciding on the relevant informations will not take long.

Select just the essential details. Trying to cram every note into your report could destroy its clarity. However, remember that the length of your report will also influence the amount of supporting detail you will need. Use as few words as possible when compiling your detailed outline. You can always refer to your notes for additional information.

The supporting details are arranged under the overall structure of the Basic Outline, as shown below. This stage is known as the Skeleton Outline.

III. Fishing
- *decline and food chain*
- *white fish eating mussels*
- *fishing equipment*

IV. Recreation
- *swimming, wading, boating, fishing*
- *shells and flesh on beaches*
- *foul water*
- *pleasure craft*
- *anglers*

V. Industry
- *also public services*
- *factories and generating stations*
- *treatment plants and fire services*
- *clogged intake pipes*
- *damaged machinery*

C. Conclusion

Skeleton Outline

A. Introduction
1. *Background (largest body, 40 m.)*
2. *Focus (zebra mussel invasion, affecting millions)*
3. *Purpose (environmental and economic impact on L. Erie)*

B. Body

I. Aquatic life
- *filtering*
- *plankton and food chain*
- *clarity and habitat*
- *spawning grounds*

II. Birds
- *diving ducks*
- *loons and cormorants*
- *gobies and zebra mussels*
- *concentrated botulism spores*
- *"Gobies becoming poison pills"*

Rough Draft

Allow time in your schedule to write up the complete report in a rough draft. Preparing the final copy will then be quick and easy, especially if you are using a computer. To help you rough out the **complete report,** the main features of the final copy are described in the pages ahead. At this stage you should check the features and format required in the final copy with your teacher.

Drafting the Introduction

The introduction "introduces" your readers to the report. It provides them with background information and it explains the focus of the report. The purpose (or question) should be spelled out at the end of the introduction — to provide the reader with a signpost, clearly indicating the direction of your journey.

Introductions are short, usually **between ten and fifteen percent** of the overall length of the report. Normally an introduction for a short report will comprise just one paragraph, although dividing your introduction into two paragraphs is quite acceptable.

Sketched out below is the introduction for the zebra mussel report. There is brief background information on the Great Lakes and the population they support and there is mention of the problems created by the zebra mussels, especially on Lake Erie — the focus of the report. And finally the purpose is spelled out. You may wish to use your research question to indicate the direction of your report, but as questions can be difficult to integrate smoothly in an introduction, it may be advisable to rephrase the question as a statement of purpose, as has been done in this example.

> The Great Lakes form the largest body of freshwater in the world and they support a population of approximately forty million people. These people rely on the lakes for drinking water, electrical power, fishing, recreation, and manufacturing. A recent invasion by a European mollusk, known as the zebra mussel, has created an ecological disaster and a multi-billion dollar headache for the millions of people who live and work in the Great Lakes basin, especially around Lake Erie. This report focuses on the impact of the zebra mussels on Lake Erie and describes how this rapidly multiplying mollusk is damaging both the environment and the economy.

Drafting the Body

The body is the longest and the most important part of the report. This is where you address the purpose of your report or answer your research question. Your response to the purpose or question represents the theme of your report — in our example, it is the impact of the zebra mussels on Lake Erie. **The body of the report is devoted entirely to developing the theme.**

Ensure that all the details are directly linked to developing the theme. Be ruthless and eliminate any information that is irrelevant. Remember that the precision and clarity of your answer is your prime objective.

Once you have completed your Skeleton Outline most of the hard slogging is over. Weaving the body together into draft form using the structure and details of your outlines is a relatively easy task. "Writer's block" is rarely a problem if you have followed a systematic research and outlining process.

Quotations are not used that frequently in short reports. If you plan to use quotations, they have to be included in the Skeleton Outline and then woven into the rough draft. To learn more about quotations turn to pages 31 and 61. You will notice that we have used a quotation in the body of our report on the next page. You need to **acknowledge** (cite or document) any quotations, ideas, or statistics that you have borrowed from your sources. Citations also have to be included in your rough draft. They are explained in detail in the pages ahead.

One of the advantages of your detailed outlines is that they provide a formula for developing your paragraphs. **Paragraphs reflect the structure of your report** and structure is a key component of clarity. In a short report of less than one thousand words, the Basic Outline will provide the paragraph structure and the Skeleton Outline will supply the supporting details for the paragraphs.

Notice how the body sections of our Skeleton Outline, reproduced below, have shaped the paragraphs of the body of our zebra mussel report on the opposite page. Each major section in the Skeleton Outline becomes a separate paragraph when drafted.

B. Body

I. Aquatic life   (Paragraph)
  - filtering
  - plankton and food chain
  - clarity and habitat
  - spawning grounds

II. Birds   (Paragraph)
  - diving ducks
  - loons and cormorants
  - gobies and zebra mussels
  - concentrated botulism spores
  - "Gobies becoming little poison pills"

III. Fishing   (Paragraph)
  - decline and food chain
  - white fish eating mussels
  - fishing equipment

IV. Recreation   (Paragraph)
  - swimming, wading, boating, fishing
  - shells and flesh on beaches
  - foul water
  - pleasure craft
  - anglers

V. Industry   (Paragraph)
  - also public services
  - factories and generating stations
  - treatment plants and fire services
  - clogged intake pipes
  - damaged machinery

One paragraph from the body of the zebra mussel report has been isolated to illustrate the key elements. The topic sentence, which states the main idea and the concluding sentence are in bold type while the remaining sentences supply the supporting details to develop the central point — "recreation."

> **The zebra mussels affect many recreational activities around Lake Erie by interfering with swimming, wading, boating, and fishing.** Bathing beaches suffer especially because the mussels prefer shallow water. Beaches are often covered with sharp shells and even decomposing mussel flesh. Furthermore, swimmers comment that the lake water frequently tastes foul because it has been filtered by millions of mussels. The hulls and motors of pleasure craft are a favourite clustering place for zebra mussels, resulting in thousands of dollars of additional maintenance and damage for the owners. Recreational anglers also complain about the declining stock and size of sport fish. **Many popular recreational activities around Lake Erie are suffering from the invasion of the zebra mussels.**

The "wagon wheel" below illustrates the structure of a paragraph. The hub **(main idea)** is supported by the spokes **(supporting details)** and the rim **(concluding sentence)** ties the paragraph together. Without sturdy supporting spokes, the wheel will collapse. Ensure that your report runs smoothly on sturdy, well constructed "wheels."

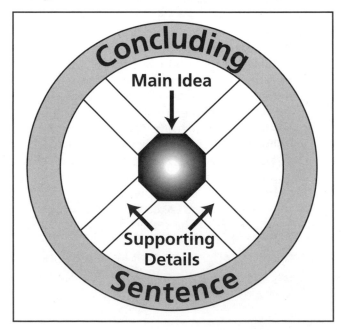

Zebra mussels can each filter about a litre of water per day. Their filtering ability is having a negative impact on aquatic life in Lake Erie. The zebra mussels filter and consume plankton and algae at the base of the food chain. Small crustaceans depend on the plankton and these crustaceans provide a primary source of food for young fish, which are then eaten by larger fish (Webber, 2001, p.15). Furthermore, the filtering ability of the zebra mussels has improved the clarity of shallow water. This has affected the habitat of small fish which were protected by slightly discoloured water. In addition, the zebra mussels have depleted fish stocks by invading their spawning grounds. The zebra mussels are disrupting the aquatic food chain with grave potential consequences for Lake Erie.

The filtering abilities of the zebra mussels and their impact on the food chain are also affecting bird life. Diving ducks are being forced to consume zebra mussels because of a shortage of fish. When filtering polluted water, the mussels accumulate toxins in their bodies, and these toxins are killing the ducks. Increasing numbers of migrating loons and cormorants are washing up dead each fall on the shores of Lake Erie. Biologists have discovered that these fish-eating birds are feeding on round gobies — another foreign invader — infected with botulism (Leahy, 2001, p.16). Zebra mussels, with high levels of filtered botulism spores in their bodies, are consumed by the gobies, who then transfer the concentrated toxins to the loons and cormorants. "Gobies are becoming little poison pills," claims biologist Jeff Robinson (Leahy, 2001, p.16). There is a risk that bird species will be decimated by the toxins that accumulate in zebra mussels, seriously affecting the biodiversity of Lake Erie.

Declining fish stocks are having a dramatic impact on both the commercial as well as the sport-fishing industries on Lake Erie. Disruptions to the food chain caused by zebra mussels are seriously affecting species, such as white fish, walleye, bass, trout, and perch. White fish are resorting to eating zebra mussels because of the lack of smaller fish on which to feed. Since the mussels are difficult to digest, the white fish mature undernourished and vulnerable to disease (Webber, 2001, p.15). Not even fishing equipment can escape the ravages of the zebra mussels: encrusted navigation buoys often sink under the weight of the mussels, dock supports deteriorate, and fishing nets are destroyed. The costs of maintaining equipment and the decline in fish stocks are having an impact on individuals, tourist resorts, and companies.

The zebra mussels affect many recreational activities around Lake Erie by interfering with swimming, wading, boating, and fishing. Bathing beaches suffer especially because the mussels prefer shallow water. Beaches are often covered with sharp shells and even decomposing mussel flesh ("Economic impacts," n.d.). Furthermore, swimmers comment that the lake water frequently tastes foul because it has been filtered by millions of mussels. The hulls and motors of pleasure craft are a favourite clustering place for zebra mussels, resulting in thousands of dollars of additional maintenance and damage for the owners. Recreational anglers also complain about the declining stock and size of sport fish. Many popular recreational activities around Lake Erie are suffering from the invasion of the zebra mussels.

Zebra mussels are inflicting major damage on manufacturing industries and public services located on both the American and Canadian shores of Lake Erie. Because the mussels prefer shallow, warmer water, they accumulate in the water intake pipes of factories, generating stations, water treatment plants, and fire protection systems. The mussels multiply rapidly and reduce the flow of water to these utilities and factories. In extreme cases they have completely clogged intake pipes, forcing the shutdown of treatment plants ("Effects," n.d.). In addition to affecting the flow of water, the mussels frequently damage machinery, such as pumps and heat exchangers. Damage and maintenance costs, such as clearing clogged pipes, impose a major financial burden on private businesses and public services on both sides of Lake Erie.

Drafting the Conclusion

The conclusion is the section where you weave together your main points and sum up the theme of your report. Do not add new information to the conclusion. New information, no matter how relevant, will confuse your readers at this late stage. If the information is important, it should be placed in the body and not added as an afterthought to the conclusion.

The conclusion usually comprises about **ten percent** of the overall length of the report. Normally only one paragraph is devoted to the conclusion in a report of this size. Although the conclusion is short, it is an important part of the report. **Remember that last impressions are usually lasting impressions.**

> In the short space of a dozen years, the zebra mussels have had a major impact on the ecology and the economy of the Great Lakes basin. Lake Erie has suffered the greatest impact because it is the shallowest and warmest of the Great Lakes. The influence of the zebra mussels starts at the base of the food chain and their impact is moving gradually higher up the chain as the mussels establish themselves more firmly in the Great Lakes. Since the economy and the ecology are so closely linked, the zebra mussels pose serious long term problems for both nature and the communities surrounding the lakes.

Once you have drafted the introduction, body, and conclusion, set aside the rough draft for a few days before you start to revise and edit. Since written expression is so important in producing a clear report, carefully study the sections on style, revising, and editing on pages 83 – 86. It is a good idea to work with a partner. You can read each other's drafts, suggesting improvements and correcting errors. Also ensure that your draft falls within the word limit assigned by the teacher.

Note that the main sections (introduction, body, conclusion) of our zebra mussel report shown in the previous four pages have already been revised and edited and are reproduced in final form. This was necessary to save space. Your draft versions will inevitably be more disorganized, but you will be pleasantly surprised at how much careful revising and editing can transform a rough draft.

Citing Sources

A common problem in writing research reports is using other peoples' ideas and information without acknowledgment. This form of copying is known as plagiarism — it is unethical and will be penalized. You must identify your sources of important information and give credit to other writers for their ideas.

The system of identifying and acknowledging your sources commonly used in social studies research involves stating the author's name and the date of publication in parentheses after the information in the text of your report. This system of citing sources was popularized by the American Psychological Association (APA). Our examples are based on the procedures of the APA system.

Providing the page reference in the citation is optional because APA only requires a page reference for a direct quotation. However, it is a good practice to indicate the precise location of all important ideas and information by providing a page number. APA recommends using the abbreviation "p." for "page" as shown in our example below. Alternatively, you may omit the "p." as shown in the example at the bottom of the page.

> Biologists have discovered that these fish-eating birds are feeding on round gobies — another foreign invader — infected with botulism (Leahy, 2001, p.16). Zebra mussels, with high levels of filtered botulism spores in their bodies, are consumed by the gobies, who then transfer the concentrated toxins to the loons and cormorants.

The reader can then refer to the list of sources at the end of the report to obtain details of the source. See Leahy in the "Bibliography" for the zebra mussel report on the opposite page for details of the source cited in the example above and below.

You can improve the readability of your report by including the author's name within the sentence and breaking up the citation, as shown in the revised example below. Omitting "p." for "page" also improves readability.

> Leahy (2001) describes how biologists have discovered that these fish-eating birds are feeding on round gobies — another foreign invader — infected with botulism (16). Zebra mussels, with high levels of filtered botulism spores in their bodies, are consumed by the gobies, who then transfer the concentrated toxins to the loons and cormorants.

Listing Sources

The brief parenthetical citations in your report must be linked to a detailed list of sources at the end of the report. To illustrate the layout for a list of sources in APA format, the final list of sources for the zebra mussel report is reproduced below.

You will need to check with your teacher whether you should list only the **sources that you cited** (or referred to) in your report or whether you should include **all the sources that proved useful** in compiling the report. Although it is more common to list all the sources used, some teachers prefer just the cited sources. This is an important issue that you must clarify with your teacher.

If your final list of sources contains only cited sources, then title it "References." On the other hand, if you include all the sources that proved useful in preparing the report, even if you did not cite all of them directly, head the list "Bibliography." The list of sources for the zebra mussel report is headed "Bibliography" because it includes not only cited sources, but other sources that helped in compiling the report.

Sources are listed in alphabetical order by author on a separate page at the end of your report. If no author is provided, use the first important word of the title to create an alphabetical list. See the examples in the zebra mussel bibliography below. **Do not number your sources.** You grouped your sources under "Books," "Articles," "Internet," and "Audio/Visual" in your Working Bibliography to help you develop a wide-ranging list of sources. Your final reference list or bibliography should not be grouped this way – it should be a **single list of sources in alphabetical order** by author or title.

When listing your sources, start with the author's last name first, followed by the initials. Next place the publication date of the source in parentheses. If no date is available, insert "N.d." in parentheses. The title of the source follows the date. If there is no author, the title will precede the date of publication. Capitalizing titles under APA guidelines is different to the traditional method of capitalization. Only capitalize the first word of the title and of the subtitle and any proper nouns.

Publication details, such as the place of publication and the publishing company, complete the entry. If a source entry extends beyond one line, indent the second and subsequent lines three spaces or a paragraph indent. You may either single or double-space sources that extend beyond one line, but individual sources must be separated by double spaces.

"Plagiarism" comes from the Latin word "plagiare" which means "to kidnap." **Plagiarism** is "kidnapping" or stealing someone else's work. It is a serious academic offence. Acknowledging the information and ideas of other writers by citing your sources carefully and by accurately listing the details at the end of your report will help you avoid charges of plagiarism.

Bibliography

Economic impacts of zebra mussel infestation. (N.d.). Retrieved April 20, 2002, from http://www. wes.army.mil/el/zebra/zmis/ ... impacts_of_zebra_infestation.htm

Effects of the zebra mussel. (N.d.). Retrieved March 16, 2002, from http://www.denison. edu/enviro/shellfish/Q3sch06.html

Fire systems now threatened by zebra mussels. (1997, April / May). *Environmental Science, 10* (2), 72-75.

Leahy, S. (2001, December 3). Lake Erie's small but toxic killers. *Maclean's, 114,* 16.

Webber, T. (2001, March 10). Food source for fish disappearing from Great Lakes. *The Telegram* (St. John's), 15.

Zorpette, G. (1996, August). Mussel mayhem. *Scientific American, 275,* 22-23.

On the following pages are examples of common types of sources listed according to APA guidelines. A selection of the more traditional print and audio-visual sources has been included below, as well as examples of online sources on the opposite page. If you are using a word processor, italicize titles, as shown in these examples. In handwritten or typed reports, titles are underlined.

Book

One Author
Bonvillain, Nancy. (1989). *The Huron.* New York: Chelsea House.

Two Authors
Strunk, W., Jr., & White, E.B. (1979). *The elements of style.* New York: Macmillan.

Multiple Authors
Colborn, T. E. et al. (1990). *Great Lakes, great legacy?* Washington: The Conservation Foundation.

Editor
Krueger, A. (Ed.). (1998). *The WTO as an international organization.* Chicago: University of Chicago Press.

No Author
The Great Lakes: An environmental atlas and resource book. (1995). Chicago: United States Environmental Protection Agency and Toronto: Environment Canada.

Corporate Author
Publication manual. (2001). Washington, DC: American Psychological Association.

Later Edition
Zinsser, W. (1998). *On writing well* (6th ed.). New York: HarperCollins.

Magazine

Leahy, S. (2001, December 3). Lake Erie's small but toxic killers. *Maclean's, 114,* 16.

Journal

Zorpette, G. (1996, August). Mussel mayhem. *Scientific American, 275,* 22-23.

Encyclopedia

Iverson, P. (2000). Navajo. In *Encyclopedia Americana* (Vol. 20, 1-5). Danbury, CT: Grolier.

Yearbook

Yapko, M.D. (1996). Repressed memories: Special report. In *Britannica book of the year 1995* (198-199). Chicago: Encyclopedia Britannica.

Video recording

Burns, K. (Director.) (1994). *The Civil War* [Videocassette]. New York: PBS.

Newspaper

Binder, D. (2000, July 11). Great Lakes face endless battle with marine invaders. *New York Times,* F4.

Government Report

International Joint Commission. (2000). *Protection of the waters of the Great Lakes.* Ottawa, ON and Washington, DC: Author.

Interview

Smales, S. (2000, June 5). Personal interview. Toronto.

Film

Costner, K. (Director). (1990). *Dances with wolves.* [Film]. New York: TIG and Orion.

Radio and Television Program

Spry-Leverton, P. (Producer) and Brier, B. (Narrator). (1998, August 27). *The Great Egyptians.* [Television]. The Learning Channel.

Art

Picasso, P. (1912). *Still life with chair-caning.* [Oil on canvas]. Musee Picasso, Paris.

Map

Physical United States. (2000). [Map]. Washington, DC: National Geographic.

CD-ROM / DVD

Discover the Great Lakes: The ecosystem of the Great Lakes-St. Lawrence. (1997). [CD-ROM]. Ottawa: Environment Canada.

Art

da Vinci, L. (1506). *The Mona Lisa*. Retrieved December 1, 2002, from http://www.louvre.fr/anglais/collec/
peint/inv0779/peint_f.htm

Book

Dickens, C. (1861). *Great Expectations*. Retrieved November 29, 2002, from http://www.bibliomania.com/
0/0/19/frameset.html

Email

Sandler, J. <judy@example.com> (2002, July 6). Re: Zebra mussels [Email to S. Conway<sconway@example.com>].

Encyclopedia

Farr, D.M.L. (2002). The Alaska Boundary Dispute. *The Canadian Encyclopedia*. Retrieved October 25, 2002, from
http://www.thecanadianencyclopedia.com/index.cfm

General Website

Archaeological Survey of Canada. (2001, July 20). *The Draper site*. Retrieved September 10, 2002, from
http://www.civilization. ca/cmc/archeo/oracles/draper/drape.htm

Journal

Menichetti, D. (1997). German policy in occupied Belgium, 1914-1918. *Essays in History, 39*. Retrieved February
9, 2002, from http://etext.lib.virginia.edu/journals/EH/EH39/menich39.html

Magazine

Tal, G. (2002, September). Learning to photograph the landscape. *Nature Photographers Online Magazine*.
Retrieved November 27, 2002, from http://www.naturephotographers. net/articles0902/gt0902-1.html

Map

The Axis Powers, 1942. (N.d.). [Map]. Retrieved September 13, 2002, from http://www.indstate.edu/gga/gga_cart/
78927.jpg

Newspaper

Schmadeke, S. (2002, November 27). Fierce flies are deployed to fight Florida fire ants. *Naples Daily News*.
Retrieved December 1, 2002, from http://www.naplesnews.com/02/11/ naples/d865261a.htm

Photograph

Simon Wiesenthal Center. (1997). *Neville Chamberlain with Adolf Hitler*. [Photograph]. Retrieved June 22, 2002,
from http://motlc.wiesenthal.com/gallery/pg18/pg7/pg18722.html

Professional Website

Crouse, M. (2002, October 18). *Citing electronic information in history papers*. Retrieved December 5, 2002, from
http://www.people.memphis.edu/~mcrouse/elcite.html

Question and Answer Database

The Chicago Manual of Style. (2002). *FAQ (and not so FAQ)*. Retrieved December 6, 2002, from http://www.
press.uchicago.edu/Misc/Chicago/cmosfaq/

Radio / Television

O'Neill, M. (1998, May 23). Chinese traditional medicines. *Quirks and Quarks*. Retrieved January 5, 2001, from
http://www.radio.cbc.ca/programs/quirks/realaud/may2398.ra

Subscription Database

Woodcock, G. (1994, August). The secrets of her success. *Quill & Quire 60*. Retrieved December 6, 2002, from
Literature Resource Center database <http://galenet.galegroup. com/servlet/LitRC>.

Title Page

Rough out your title page as part of the drafting process. Phrase your title so that it clearly indicates to the reader the **focus of your report.** Use a subtitle only if it helps clarify the title. Normally the title is not stated in question form. The following information is usually required on title pages:

- Title
- Name
- Class/Subject
- Teacher
- Date

It is unlikely that you will use a table of contents, subheadings, illustrations, or an appendix in a short report of less than a thousand words, but check all requirements, including the marking criteria, again with your teacher. Ensure that you have included **all the sections and features** of your report in the rough draft and arrange them in the correct order: title page → introduction → body → conclusion → sources.

Once you have finished revising and editing, reread the draft slowly, polishing and fine tuning it. Before starting the final copy, confirm with your teacher the format for laying it out.

Final Copy

If you have composed a comprehensive rough draft and reviewed it thoroughly, preparing the final copy will be quick and easy, especially if you use a computer. Remember that the copy you submit to your teacher represents just the tip of the iceberg. Frequently, that ten percent of the iceberg above the water counts for 100 percent of the mark, so take special care in the way you assemble the final copy.

Ensure that your report is legibly written or clearly typed. Typed assignments are double-spaced but handwritten assignments may be single or double-spaced depending on your teacher's preference. Check with your teacher whether your report should be in a folder and if the pages should be stapled.

Proofread your report meticulously for errors. Ask a member of your group to do a second proofreading. Frequent errors create a poor impression and will have a negative effect on the evaluation. On the other hand, a neat, orderly, and error-free assignment will have a positive impact on the reader.

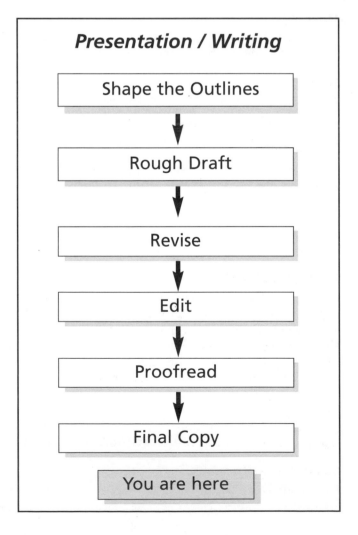

The Impact of the Zebra Mussels on Lake Erie

Raymond Wade
Geography 1A

Ms Helen Thexton
20 May 2002

Presentation / Writing

Shape the Outlines

Rough Draft

Revise

Edit

Proofread

Final Copy

You are here

3 ◆ Writing about Literature

In English classes you will be exposed to various types of writing. Some assignments will focus on expository reports, others will engage you in creative writing, and you will also be required to write essays on the literary works you are studying. An essay on a work of literature will lead you into the realm of interpretation and analysis. Such an essay allows you to develop your own point of view; at the same time, it requires that you support that point of view or interpretation with a combination of thoughtful observations and relevant evidence from the text.

An essay is not a narrative, a descriptive composition, or a plot summary. An **essay has a point of view or thesis** — that is the central feature of an essay and what distinguishes it from an expository report or a piece of creative writing.

When writing essays on literary works, such as plays, poems, short stories, and novels, you are seldom required to do research in secondary sources. It is **your** interpretation of the primary text that the teacher wants to read, not interpretations by literary critics. It is your insights and your reactions that are important.

In high school you will increasingly be expected to show how the meaning of a work of literature is shaped by the author's use of literary (or stylistic) techniques, such as characterization, plot, mood, and setting. For example, rather than summarizing the plot of a novel or describing its main characters, your teacher will ask you to explain how these and other literary devices serve to shape the novel's meaning.

Three common approaches used by teachers to assign essays on works of literature are described in this chapter. These approaches can be used with all literary genres. You will discover that the same basic process underlies all three of the sample assignments.

ASSIGNMENT 1

Let us assume that you are studying Ernest Buckler's short story, "Long, Long After School," in class. After reading the story, you have had the opportunity to discuss it in small groups. The teacher then assigned "Long, Long After School" as the topic for an essay. Note that the assignment is an **essay.** You will not be summarizing the short story or detailing the life of Ernest Buckler. You will be analyzing and interpreting the short story and developing a point of view or thesis in response to a question.

The teacher has provided a list of questions on the story. You are required to select one question and write a response of 800–900 words. No secondary sources are to be used for the essay. Formulating a title will also be your responsibility.

Before launching into the assignment, make sure that you understand the specific requirements for the essay. Clarify the following questions and issues with your teacher **before** you start.

- When is it due?
- Are notes and drafts due at specific times?
- Will there be class time to work on the project?
- How will it be marked?
- How should the essay be structured?

A month has been allocated to the project. You will have to plan a schedule so that you can complete the essay by the deadline. You should allow about half the time for the preparation or pre-writing and the other half for composing and writing the essay. **Organize your time** so that you do not have to rush to finish the essay at the last minute. Time-management is a valuable life-skill.

Long, Long After School

I ran into Wes Holman the very day I was collecting for Miss Tretheway's flowers. But it never came into my head to ask him for a contribution.

Miss Tretheway had taught grade three in our town for exactly fifty years. She had died the night before in her sleep. As chairman of the school board I had thought it would be fitting if all the grade three alumni who were still around made up enough money to get a really handsome "piece." She had no relatives. If I'd given it an instant's consideration I'd have known that Wes himself must have been in grade three some time or other; but I didn't.

Wes was just coming through the cemetery gate as I was going in. Wes "looks after" the cemetery, and I sometimes take a short cut through it on my way to work. I should say that Wes is our local "character." His tiny house up behind the ballpark is furnished with almost nothing but books, and he can quote anyone from Seneca to Henry James. But that's his job: caretaker-about-town.

When I spoke to him about Miss Tretheway, a curious change came into his face. You couldn't say that he turned pale, but his stillness was quite different from the conventional one on such occasions. I had expected him to come out with some quote or other, but he didn't say a word.

He didn't go to her funeral. But he sent her flowers of his own. Or brought them, rather. The following day, when I took the shortcut again, I surprised him on his knees placing them.

His little bunch of flowers was the most incongruous thing you could imagine. It was a corsage. A corsage of simple flowers, such as a young boy sends his girl for her first formal dance. And more incongruous than its presence in the circumstance of death was its connection with Miss Tretheway herself. I'm quite sure that Miss Tretheway never once had a beau send her flowers, that she had never been to a dance in her whole life.

I suppose it would never have occurred to me to question any one but Wes about his motive for doing a thing like that. But I asked Wes about it with no thought of rudeness whatever. Wes's privacy seemed to be everyone's property. There was probably a little self-conscious democracy in the gesture when we talked to him at all.

"She was so beautiful," he answered me, as if no other explanation was needed.

That was plainly ridiculous. That Miss Tretheway was a fine person for having spent a lifetime in small, unheralded services could not be disputed – but obviously she hadn't ever been beautiful. Her sturdy plainness was never transfigured, not even for an instant, by the echo of anything winsomer which had faded. Her eyes had never been very blue, her skin very pink, or her hair very brown. She wasn't very anything. Her heart might have been headlong (I think now that it was), but there was always that curious precision and economy in her face which lacks altogether the grain of helter-skelter necessary to any kind of charm. In short, even when she'd been a girl, she'd been the sort of girl whose slightest eagerness, more than if she were ugly or old, a young man automatically shies away from.

"But, Wes," I said half-joking, "she wasn't beautiful. What made you say that?"

His story went something like this. He told it with a kind of dogged, confessional earnestness. I guess he'd come to figure that whenever we asked him a personal question he might as well sat-

isfy our curiosity completely, first as last.

"Perhaps you remember how the kids used to tease me at school," he said. (I didn't. I guess those things stick in your mind according to which end of the teasing you happen to be on.) "If the boys would be telling some joke with words in it to giggle over, they'd look at me and say, 'Shhh . . . Wes is blushing.' Or if we were all climbing up the ladder to the big beams in Hogan's stable, they'd say 'Look at Wes. He's so scared he's turning pale.' Do you remember the night you steered your sled into mine, going down Parker hill?"

"No," I said. "Did I do it on purpose?"

"I don't know," Wes said. "Maybe you didn't. I thought you did."

Maybe I did. I don't remember.

"I was taking Mrs. Banks's wash home on my sled, and you were coasting down the hill. The basket upset and all the things fell out on the snow. Don't you remember . . . Miss Tretheway came along and you all ran. She helped me pick up the stuff and shake the snow off it. She went with me right to Mrs. Banks's door and told her what had happened. I could never have made Mrs. Banks believe I didn't upset the stuff myself."

"I'm sorry," I said. *I probably had done it on purpose.*

"That's all right," he said. "I didn't mind the boys so much. It was the girls. You can't hit a girl. There just wasn't anything I could do about the girls. One day Miss Tretheway was showing us a new game in the schoolyard. I don't remember exactly how it went, but that one where we all made a big circle and someone stood in the centre. I put my hand out to close up the ring with the biggest Banks girl, but she wouldn't take it. She said, 'Your hands are dirty.' Miss Tretheway made us both hold out our hands. She said, 'Why, Marilyn, Wes's hands are much cleaner than your's. Maybe Wes doesn't like to get his hands dirty, did you ever think about that?' She took Marilyn's place herself. Her hands felt safe and warm, I remember . . . and I guess that's the first day I thought she was beautiful."

"I see," I said.

I did, and yet I didn't. The Wes I remember would hate anything with the suggestion of teacher's pet about it. The only Wes I could seem to remember was the Wes of adolescence: the tough guy with the chip on his shoulder.

He was coming to that but he stuck in an odd parenthesis first. "Did you ever notice Miss Tretheway," he said, "when . . . well, the other teachers would be talking in the hall about the dances they'd been to over the weekend? Or when she'd be telling some kid a story after school and the kid would run off right in the middle of a sentence when she saw her mother coming to pick her up?"

"No," I said. "Why? What about it?"

"Oh, nothing, I guess." He drew a deep breath. "Anyway, I decided I'd be stronger and I'd study harder than anyone. And I was, wasn't I? I did. Do you remember the year they voted me the best all-round student in High School?" (I didn't. It must have been after I'd graduated.) "I guess I just can't remember how happy I was about that. I guess I was so happy I could believe anything. That must have been why I let the boys coax me into going to the closing dance." He smiled. "I thought since they'd voted for me . . . but you can't legislate against a girl's glance."

Those were his exact words. Maybe he'd read them somewhere. Maybe they were his own. I don't know. But it was the kind of remark which had built up his quaint reputation as the town philosopher.

"I didn't want to go out on the dance floor," he said. "I'd never danced a foxtrot or anything. The girls all had on their evening dresses, and somehow they looked different altogether. They looked as if they wouldn't recognize themselves in their day clothes. Anyway, the boys grabbed hold of me and made me get into a Paul Jones. I was next to Toby Wenford in the big ring. Jane Evans was right opposite me when the music stopped, but she danced with Toby instead – and the girl next to Jane just glanced at me and then went and sat down. I guess it was a pretty foolish thing to do, but I went down in the basement and drove my fist through a window."

"Is that the scar?" I said. I couldn't think of anything else to say.

"Oh, it was a lot worse than that," he said. He pulled up his sleeve and traced the faint sickle of the scar way up his arm. "You can hardly see it now. But I almost bled to death right there. I guess I might have, if it hadn't been for Miss Tretheway."

"Oh?" I said. "How's that?"

"You see, they didn't have any plasma around in bottles then," he said, "and in those days no one felt too comfortable about having his blood siphoned off. I guess no one felt like taking any chances for me, anyway. Mother said I could have hers, but hers wasn't right. Mine's that odd type – three, isn't it? Miss Tretheway was three, too . . . and that's funny; because only seven percent of people have it. She gave me a whole quart, just as soon as she found out that hers would match."

"I see," I said. So that was it. And yet I had a feeling that wasn't it – not quite.

"She used to come to see me everyday," he said. "She used to bring me books. Did you know that books . . . well, that for anyone like me that's the only way you can . . . ?" He hesitated, and I knew that wasn't quite it either.

Not until he spoke again, when he spoke so differently, was I sure that only now was he coming to the real thing.

"Do you know what Miss Tretheway said when I thanked her for the transfusion?" he said. "She made a joke of it. She said: 'I didn't know whether an old maid's blood would be any good to a fine young specimen like you, Wes, or not.' The thing I always remember, I knew that was the first time she'd ever called herself an old maid to anyone, and really felt like laughing. And I remember what I said. I said: 'Miss Tretheway, you're making me blush.' And do you know, that was the very first time I'd ever been able to say that, and laugh, myself."

There was quite a long silence.

"She was beautiful," he added softly. "She was a real lady." The cemetery is right next to the river. I looked down the river where the cold December water lapped at the jagged ice thrown up on the banks, and I thought about a boy the colour of whose skin was such that he could never blush, and I thought about a girl who had never been asked to dance. I thought about the corsage. My curiosity was quite satisfied. But somehow I myself had never felt less beautiful, or less of a gentleman.

Ernest Buckler.

Preparation

You have read and discussed the story in class; the teacher has set the question; you are not required to use any other sources. Therefore, much of the preliminary preparation (or pre-writing) has already been done. Let us assume that you choose the following question from the list of questions:

"How does the author use literary devices, such as characterization, symbolism, and dialogue to convey the major themes in the story?"

With a clear sense of direction provided by the question, you are now ready to start the **preparatory reading.** Although you have read and discussed the story already, you did not at that stage have a question to provide you with focus and direction. Read the story again carefully, reflecting this time on the question as you read. You are not taking detailed notes at this stage — you are "preparing" yourself for the next stage: analyzing the short story and recording the ideas and examples needed to answer the question.

Unlike a report, an essay does not usually lend itself to a Working Outline. You do not need to plan a tentative structure at this stage. The structure will be developed later in the process. Instead, concentrate on your reactions and responses to the question as you read the story and jot down any ideas and suggestions in your *I.Q. Journal.*

After you have completed the preparatory reading, you are ready to subject the story to a detailed analysis in the light of your question. Your task is to answer the question — that is the sole purpose of the assignment and your sole responsibility. **Your answer will form your thesis or point of view.**

Since you cannot remember everything that you read, especially in lengthy literary works, a **systematic method** for recording your ideas and examples is essential. The notepaper method described here differs slightly from the method used in the report because it is not based on a Working Outline.

Set up your notepaper recording system by ruling a right-hand margin of 2-3 cm on the front side of the page only, as shown below. (These pages do not have headings like those used in the report.) Prepare a number of pages in advance so that you have a supply of notepaper for your notes. If you are using a computer, you can create "electronic notepaper" by setting up a file for your notes in your word processor (Microsoft *Word* or Corel *WordPerfect*). Set up your "page" by creating a table with three columns, as shown here.

Preparation / Pre-writing

```
Topic
  ↓
Focus          Set
  ↓            by
Purpose /      teacher
Question
  ↓
Preparatory Reading
  ↓
[You are here]
  ↓
Record Examples
```

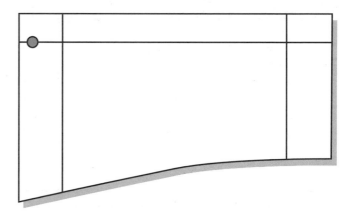

As you read through "Long, Long After School," you will be searching for ideas and examples that will help you answer your question ("How does the author use literary devices, such as characterization, symbolism, and dialogue to convey the major themes in the story?")

On page 24 you notice a reference to flowers and you may decide that the author has used flowers as symbols of an important theme. Since this point is relevant to your question, you record it in the centre column of your notepaper, as shown in the diagram below. You must also identify the precise location of the note in the short story by inserting the page number in the left-hand margin.

Continue reading through the short story, searching for ideas and examples that will help you develop an answer to your question. Then record your responses and examples on notepaper or on a computer, as just explained. Further, on page 24 Wes describes Miss Tretheway as being "beautiful." Since this comment by Wes is important to the characterization of Miss Tretheway, you make a note of it. The narrator's response to this comment by Wes is also important because it accentuates Miss Tretheway's absence of physical attractiveness; her appearance blinds the narrator to her 'inner beauty,' a quality that he finally recognizes after listening to Wes's narrative.

Page	Note or quotation
24	"His little bunch of flowers was the most incongruous thing you could imagine. It was a corsage. A corsage of simple flowers, such as a boy sends his girl for her first formal dance." (Contrast the symbolic value of this simple corsage to the "handsome 'piece'" donated by the narrator.)

| Page number | Note or quotation |

| 24 | "She was so beautiful," he answered me. (A characteristic of Miss T. that becomes apparent as the story unfolds.) |
| 24 | " . . . Miss T. was a fine person . . . but obviously she hadn't ever been beautiful." (The narrator learns after his dialogue with Wes that Miss T. |

possessed a 'beauty' that he was unable to recognize because of his lack of tolerance for those who were different.)

Copy your examples from the text accurately, using quotation marks to indicate what part of your note is quoted directly from the text. Use an ellipsis (three spaced periods) to indicate where you have omitted words from the original. If possible, always include a bracketed comment on a quoted note.

In recording the notes in the previous column, you have:

- Discovered examples relevant to your question.

- Recorded the details in note and/or quotation form.

- Indicated the page reference for each note.

The **whole process** of recording the ideas and the evidence needed to develop an answer to your question is covered in the three steps above.

Analysis is breaking something down into its smaller parts. Analysis of a literary work involves examining the text carefully in order to identify those themes and literary devices that are pertinent to your question. After selecting examples from the text that illustrate the themes and devices, record these examples as explained in the previous column. Notice how this selection of relevant examples is **guided by the question** which also guides your analysis.

Always ask yourself how the examples that you are noting will be relevant to developing an answer to your question. If your essay is based on a short literary work, such as, "Long, Long After School," reread the text two or three times to search for ideas, insights, and examples that will help answer the question.

Once you have filled one page of notepaper, start another. Do not write on the reverse side of the page. Writing on one side of the page only and leaving a line between each note will allow you to separate all your notes later during the outlining and structuring process. If you are using a word processor, be sure to leave a line between each note.

Since analyzing the text and making notes on it is an important stage in preparing your essay, allow **enough time** in your schedule to do the analysis thoroughly. Keep these points in mind:

- Copy quotations accurately and place them in quotation marks with page references.

- Summarize or paraphrase details in your own words, where necessary.

- Be clear and accurate when making your notes.

- Insert your own ideas, questions, and comments in your notes.

- Ensure that your notes are relevant to the question.

Presentation

Once you have completed analyzing the text and recording your ideas and examples, you can start shaping your answer to the question. **Your answer or response represents your thesis or point of view.** The clarity of your thesis is largely determined by the style of your expression and the structure of your answer. As in the report, the ABC formula also provides an effective structure for an essay.

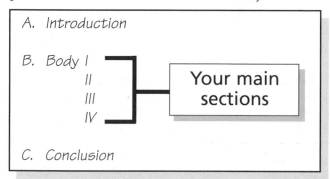

```
A. Introduction

B. Body I ┐
      II  ├──  Your main
      III │      sections
      IV  ┘

C. Conclusion
```

It is impossible to write the final copy straight from your notes. Shaping the structure of the essay is your first task. Unlike the report, where the research was based on a Working Outline, our notes on "Long, Long After School" were not organized according to an outline. Your next step is to create **an outline that imposes order on the ideas and examples in your notes.**

Read through your notes (paper or electronic) focusing on the question ("How does the author use literary devices, such as characterization, symbolism, and dialogue to convey the major themes in the story?"). Try to isolate the main factors around which you can structure your answer. Sometimes, as in our example, the question will suggest the structure for the body. This list of main factors forms the Basic Outline, as shown below.

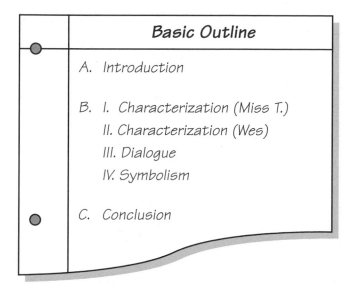

Basic Outline

A. Introduction

B. I. Characterization (Miss T.)
   II. Characterization (Wes)
   III. Dialogue
   IV. Symbolism

C. Conclusion

Separate the individual notes with scissors — that is why you wrote on one side of the paper only. Read through your separated note slips and then group them according to the sections of the Basic Outline. The next step is to number each group of notes according to the Basic Outline. Use the empty right-hand column to indicate the numbered section of the Basic Outline, as shown below. For instance, all notes dealing with symbolism are labelled "IV" because "Symbolism" is section IV of the Basic Outline shown in the previous column. Likewise all notes dealing with the character of Wes in the story are labelled "II" because "Characterization (Wes)" is section II of the Basic Outline. Use paper clips to group the notepaper strips.

| 24 | "His little bunch of flowers was the most incongruous thing you could imagine." (Ironically, they symbolize much more than the narrator's large bouquet.) | IV |

| 25 | "Do you remember the year they voted me the best all-round student in High School?" (Wes is determined to overcome racial prejudice by working hard at being the best.) | II |

If you used a computer to record your notes, you could print your notes and cut and group them as just explained for the paper method. Alternatively, you can create separate files for each section of the Basic Outline and then transfer the individual notes to the appropriate file by cutting and pasting. Your electronic notes will now be grouped in separate files according to the sections of the Basic Outline.

Some notes will not fit into the sections of the body or the introduction. Do not be concerned if you cannot use all of your notes. They are not wasted because even the rejected notes have helped you develop a better understanding of your response to the question.

There is no magic number of sections in the body of the Basic Outline — from three to six sections will handle most questions. But you must ensure that **all the sections** directly address the question. Remember that your sole responsibility is to answer the question.

Developing a convincing answer to your question will require **supporting it with ideas and examples** drawn from your notes. Take one section of your notes at a time and read through the notes carefully, selecting the essential supporting details. This is not a long process because you have a good understanding of your notes by now. The supporting details are then organized under the overall structure of the Basic Outline, as demonstrated below. This stage is known as the Skeleton Outline.

Skeleton Outline

A. Introduction   (Paragraph)
  - thesis statement

B. I.   Characterization   (Paragraph)
(Miss T.)
  - courageous
  - plain "old maid"
  - beautiful 'on the inside'
  - understanding and compassionate

II.   Characterization   (Paragraph)
(Wes)
  - suffers from prejudice
  - response to injustice
  - pain makes him more sensitive

III. Dialogue   (Paragraph)
  - point of view from which story told
  - Wes's skin colour

  - Miss T's donation of blood
  - narrator affected by dialogue
    with Wes

IV. Symbolism   (Paragraph)
  - donation of blood
  - books and greater understanding
  - flowers

C. Conclusion   (Paragraph)

Allow time in your schedule **to rough out the complete essay** in a preliminary draft. If the essay is disjointed, you may wish to change the order of the sections in the body. Rearrange them in a sequence that best develops your thesis. An ascending order of interest and importance for the main sections usually works best. With a detailed Skeleton Outline mapped out, preparing a rough draft will be quick and easy, especially if you are using a computer.

One of the advantages of preparing detailed outlines for your reports and essays is that they provide a formula for developing your paragraphs. **Paragraphs play a key role in shaping the clarity of your answers.** A paragraph is a series of sentences that addresses one major idea or step in developing the thesis of your essay. A topic sentence, usually placed at the beginning, introduces the paragraph and clearly states the central idea. The sentences that follow provide the supporting details for the main idea of the paragraph. A concluding sentence sums up the paragraph and re-establishes the main point. Do you remember the "wagon wheel" on page 16?

The number of paragraphs for an essay (or a report) cannot be determined in advance. Every essay is unique and the paragraph structure will flow from your question, your analysis, your thinking, your outlines, and the length of the essay. **Only you** can determine the ideal number of paragraphs that will best develop your thesis. It is unlikely, however, that only two paragraphs in the body will provide a sturdy structure on which to build your essay. At least three body paragraphs, and no more than six, will provide a solid base for an essay of less than a thousand words.

Introductions for essays on literary works tend to be shorter than introductions for reports. For example, there is usually no background information in a short essay on a literary text. Often the question is also omitted. Generating questions for literary analysis is more complex than designing questions for social studies reports and essays. Consequently some teachers may set the questions initially, such as our essay on "Long, Long After School." Where the questions have been set, a clear, precise title will indicate to the teacher the question you selected from the prescribed list.

The key feature of the introduction is to state your response to the question and to convey to the reader the line of argument you will pursue. This is commonly known as the **thesis statement.** In the introduction to our essay on "Long, Long After School" the major themes are clearly stated and then linked with the devices of characterization, dialogue, and symbolism.

In Ernest Buckler's short story, "Long, Long After School," the main theme of self-knowledge gradually emerges through the use of characterization, dialogue, and symbolism. The story also depicts the themes of love and tolerance. The narrator learns that the appearance of people can be deceiving and that true beauty comes from a person's character and not from physical looks. Racism lurks in the attitudes of the majority white community which teases, excludes, and takes for granted a black boy who is in the minority in the town. Love expresses itself in generous and kind deeds, such as Miss Tretheway's gift of her own blood to save the life of Wes, the injured black student. Most important, however, is that the narrator emerges from his egotistical blindness and discovers the true meaning of love and tolerance.

The body of the essay is the longest and the most important section. **The sole function of the body is to develop and substantiate your thesis.** Therefore, take special care to ensure that all the ideas and examples in the body of your essay explicitly support and reinforce your thesis.

The concluding paragraph sums up the major supporting points and provides the essay with a sense of closure. Do not add any new information or ideas in the conclusion. All evidence relevant to the thesis must be included in the body of the essay.

In composing your responses to questions on literary works, you will need to refer to the texts to illustrate your interpretations and ideas. Sometimes you will paraphrase information but frequently you will quote directly from the text. Direct quotations from the primary text are more common in essays on literary works than social studies reports and essays.

In essays of less than a thousand words most of your quotations will be fairly short. Quotations of less than forty words should be integrated as naturally and as smoothly as possible into your essay and enclosed within quotation marks, as shown below. Longer quotations, also known as block quotations, are indented and separated from the text. See page 61 for details on using block quotations.

Miss Tretheway pointed out to Marilyn that "Wes's hands are much cleaner than yours. Maybe Wes doesn't like to get his hands dirty."

The narrator's flowers may seem more appropriate than Wes's small corsage "such as a young boy sends his girl for her first formal dance."

You must also indicate the location of material that you have used to write your essay. Since your essays on literary works will be based solely on the primary text initially, the procedure for citing your sources will be slightly different to the APA parenthetical method described earlier for the report. As you are using only one source, it will not be necessary to mention the title of the source or the author in the citation. Just the page reference is cited in parentheses, as shown in the sample essay on pages 32–33. This parenthetical documentation style, developed by the Modern Language Association (MLA), is widely used in writing essays on literature. It is described in detail on pages 116–18.

When you plan your schedule, allow time to set the rough draft aside for a few days before you start to revise and edit. Getting a little "distance" from the draft will sharpen your editorial eye. Refer to the section on style, revising, and editing on pages 83–86 for additional advice. The time spent on revising and editing is time well spent. Ernest Hemingway is reputed to have rewritten the ending to *A Farewell to Arms* thirty-nine times before he was satisfied.

Before starting the final copy, check all the requirements, such as the layout and also the marking criteria, with your teacher again. With a revised and edited rough draft, you will find preparing the final copy a quick and painless task, especially if you are using a word processor. All the hard work will have paid off. Do not forget to **proofread** your essay before submitting it.

Readers see your title page first, so set it up in a neat and orderly fashion, as shown opposite. The title, precisely and concisely phrased, must indicate clearly to the reader the focus of your essay. Questions and thesis statements are not substitutes for titles.

The sample essay on "Long, Long After School" is shown in final format opposite. It follows the paragraph structure (with supporting details) illustrated in the Skeleton Outline on page 30. It is not necessary to devote a separate page to listing the single primary text on which the essay was based. If you have space at the end of the essay, insert the "Work Cited" as shown.

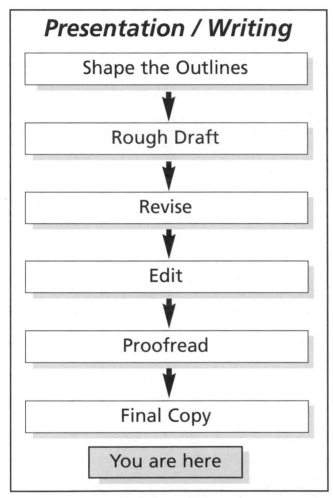

Presentation / Writing

Shape the Outlines

↓

Rough Draft

↓

Revise

↓

Edit

↓

Proofread

↓

Final Copy

You are here

The process for preparing and presenting a report and an essay on a work of literature is fundamentally the same. If you have developed a pathway for your reports and essays, you can make minor modifications in the process that will enable you to tackle a variety of assignments. The pathways (or routes) shown on page 2 might vary slightly, but whether you are writing an 800 word essay on a single work of literature, an 800 word research report in geography, or a 2000 word term paper in history, the destination is the same: **a clear, coherent presentation of your response to the question.**

Characterization, Dialogue, and Symbolism in "Long, Long After School"

Olivia McNee
English 1E

N. Jowett
15 May 2002

In Ernest Buckler's short story, "Long, Long After School," the main theme of self-knowledge gradually emerges through the use of characterization, dialogue, and symbolism. The story also depicts the themes of love and tolerance. The narrator learns that the appearance of people can be deceiving and that true beauty comes from a person's character and not from physical looks. Racism lurks in the attitudes of the majority white community which teases, excludes, and takes for granted a black boy who is in the minority in the town. Love expresses itself in generous and kind deeds, such as Miss Tretheway's gift of her own blood to save the life of Wes, the injured black student. Most important, however, is that the narrator emerges from his egotistical blindness and discovers the true meaning of love and tolerance.

Miss Tretheway shows courage in being kind to Wes when she could have ignored him and treated him as an outcast just as so many others in the community did. The narrator's characterization of the grade three teacher was the same as the rest of the town's — she was plain and "hadn't ever been beautiful" (24). However, the narrator realizes, after hearing Wes's story, that she really was beautiful. Unlike the majority of the community, she did not take Wes for granted nor was she racist. During a game in the schoolyard, one of Wes's classmates refused to hold his hand because she thought that she might get her hand dirty. Miss Tretheway points out to Marilyn that "Wes's hands are much cleaner than yours. Maybe Wes doesn't like to get his hands dirty" (25). This act of understanding and compassion foreshadows Miss Tretheway's donation of blood to Wes. Miss Tretheway was courageous enough to accept Wes in an intolerant community and repeatedly took his side when he was subjected to prejudice.

The characterization of Wes, who suffers from the prejudice of his peers but is treated with kindness by Miss Tretheway, is important in revealing the story's major themes. Determined to be accepted by the other students, Wes works hard at school. Despite becoming the top student in the school, he is rejected by the girls at the school's closing dance. This act of intolerance by the girls fuels his anger, a natural response from a sensitive boy who has suffered a grave injustice. He was so hurt by this act that he ". . . drove [his] fist through a window" (26) and almost bled to death. It is Miss Tretheway who tends to his wound and calms him. The pain that Wes suffers by being an outcast helps him understand the beauty that lies within Miss Tretheway, a quality of which the narrator, untouched by prejudice, is oblivious.

Most of the story, told from the narrator's point of view, is in the form of a dialogue. During the course of the dialogue between Wes and the narrator, the reader is unaware of the colour of Wes's skin, but is aware that the narrator shares the opinions of the rest of the town about Wes and Miss Trethewey. However, as the conversation between Wes and the narrator continues, the narrator begins to empathize with both Miss Trethewey and Wes. In several incidents described by Wes, Miss Trethewey showed signs of love towards Wes. For example, after Miss Trethewey donated blood to Wes, she remarked to him: "I

didn't know whether an old maid's blood would be any good to a fine young specimen like you, Wes, or not" (26). Through the telling of such events Wes makes Miss Trethewey's good humour and compassion apparent to the narrator as well as the reader. As the dialogue proceeds, the narrator's view of Miss Trethewey changes as he begins to appreciate her real beauty.

Since "Long, Long After School" is a relatively short work, the author uses symbolism to strengthen the themes of the story. The theme of love is symbolized by Miss Trethewey's donation of blood to Wes. She gave him life which is an expression of love. While Wes was recovering from his injury, she visited him and brought him books, symbolizing education and the opening up of other worlds for him. The narrator buys a "handsome piece" (24) for Miss Trethewey's funeral, believing that it was a suitable gesture, although he did not put much thought into it. The narrator's flowers may seem more appropriate than Wes's small corsage "such as a young boy sends his girl for her first formal dance" (24). But when, at the end of the story, the narrator realizes how much thought and emotion went into Wes's simple flowers, his "handsome piece" seemed trivial in comparison.

The title of the story, "Long, Long After School," makes reference to "school," a place in our society where we are supposed to learn. The narrator only learns important qualities of humanity later in life, qualities that he should have learned at school. He learns to be more tolerant and understanding of those who are different. He also learns that love is possible in unlikely circumstances. The story of Wes and Miss Trethewey has given him a deeper understanding of himself and of others.

Work Cited

Buckler, Ernest. "Long, Long After School." *Sightlines 9.* Ed. Alice Barlow-Kedves et al. Toronto: Prentice Hall Ginn, 1999. 112-116.

ASSIGNMENT 2

Frequently your teachers will ask you to prepare an essay in advance and then write it as an in-class assignment. You may be allowed to use notes and/or outlines or you may be required to write the essay without access to notes and outlines.

Let us assume that you are studying the theme of racism in various works of literature. Your teacher has assigned Harper Lee's anti-racist novel, *To Kill a Mockingbird,* as the topic for a short essay of 600–700 words. The teacher has provided a list of questions from which you have to select one. No secondary sources are to be used for the essay. The essay will be prepared in advance and written as an in-class assignment. You may bring a Skeleton Outline into class but no notes are permitted. No direct quotations or citations are required in the answer.

A month has been allocated for the project and some class and homework time will be set aside for the reading and preparation. No class or group discussions on the novel will take place — this will be a solo effort. Plan your schedule for the different stages so that you are thoroughly prepared to write a top notch final copy. Clarify any concerns or questions with your teacher before getting started.

Since the question has been set and because you are not required to use any other sources, much of the preliminary preparation (or pre-writing) has been eliminated. Let us assume that you choose the following question: "How does the narrator of *To Kill a Mockingbird,* Scout Finch, learn to distinguish between appearance and reality?"

Once again, **the question provides you with a clear sense of direction.** After your first reading of *To Kill a Mockingbird* — the preparatory reading — you must then subject the novel to detailed analysis in the light of the question. This will involve a more careful reading of the text in order to select and record the ideas and examples that will help you develop your response to the question. Like all essays, your response represents your thesis or point of view. There is no need to develop a Working Outline; delay the structuring until you create the Basic and Skeleton outlines.

You can use either notepaper or "electronic notepaper" for your notes, as explained earlier. Although there are some differences (length of the texts and nature of the final essay), the preparation or pre-writing process is almost identical to the process used in the short story essay as outlined on page 27.

The process for composing your answer or thesis is also identical to the method described for the short story essay. The first step is to impose order on your notes by developing a Basic Outline and then a Skeleton Outline. **The detailed outlines will again provide the paragraph structure and supply the supporting details,** as demonstrated below. If you rough out a draft in advance, writing the final copy in class will be a rewarding, not an intimidating, experience.

Basic Outline

A. Introduction

B. I. Boo Radley

   II. Mrs. Dubose

   III. Tom Robinson's trial

C. Conclusion

Skeleton Outline

A. Introduction   (Paragraph)
- thesis statement

B. I. Boo Radley   (Paragraph)
- seen as a monster
- how the children mock him
- examples of Boo's kindness

   II. Mrs. Dubose   (Paragraph)
- seen as a wicked woman
- Jem's revenge
- the children's punishment
- the truth about Mrs. Dubose

   III. Tom Robinson's trial   (Paragraph)
- the jury's prejudice
- Scout and Jem's reaction
- Tom as the Mockingbird
- the townspeople's racism
- Tom killed

C. Conclusion   (Paragraph)

In *To Kill a Mockingbird*, Harper Lee uses the narrative form of an older woman reflecting on her childhood memories in order to show how she, as a young girl, learns from three events to discriminate between what appears to be true and what is actually true. She, nicknamed Scout, and her older brother, Jem, misjudge the true nature of their neighbours, Boo Radley and Mrs. Dubose. They also learn from the trial of Tom Robinson to look beyond the surface in order to see the racism underlying community life in Maycomb County.

At the beginning of the novel, the children's lives are taken up with routine activities, such as playing in the treehouse on their property and getting to know a neighbour, Dill, who is visiting for the summer. However, their main source of amusement is their mysterious neighbour, Boo Radley. At first, the children are terrified by the grotesque image of Boo which is created by the townspeople. Scout and Jem entertain themselves by re-enacting the horrid tales told to them about Boo by the town's gossip, Miss Stephanie Crawford. All the while Boo, without the children knowing, watches over them from afar as their protector. With the passage of time, evidence of Boo's kindness towards the children becomes clear, such as when he returns Jem's pants, neatly folded. At the end of the novel he saves Scout from the drunken Mr. Ewell. What had once been an obvious truth to the children is now unveiled as a complete lie. Boo, the mysterious monster, is really a kind and gentle man who, because of his genuine concern for the children, ends up saving Scout's life.

Another revelation to the children is the true nature of Mrs. Dubose, at the outset a wicked woman in their estimation. She constantly torments the children, yelling obscenities at them from across the street. After months of misery, Jem finally cracks. In a blind rage he lashes out at her by shredding her prized camellias to pieces. As punishment Atticus Finch, their father, makes Jem and Scout read to Mrs. Dubose every day even though she continues to abuse them. They are only released from their punishment after Mrs Dubose dies some months later. Atticus explains to the children that during all this time Mrs. Dubose had been courageously battling her addiction to morphine and that their reading had helped her. Her apparent wickedness covered up, as Atticus explains, the greatest courage of all — that although something seems impossible, you should never give up. Mrs. Dubose died free of her addiction to morphine.

Perhaps the greatest revelation of truth for the children is the racist attitude of the town. Tom Robinson, who is black, is accused of raping a white girl, Mayella Ewell. Tom's lawyer, Atticus Finch, clearly establishes his innocence. However, the all-white jury are too set in their views to see past their bigotry and they find Tom guilty. Both children, heartbroken and angry over the injustice, are left disillusioned about the reality of the world in which they live. Tom is one of the few characters who truly embodies the image of the Mockingbird, an innocent creature whose sole intention is to produce joy and do good in the world. In comparison, the townspeople appear hateful and vengeful. For example, Mr. Cunningham, seemingly a quiet, shy, and decent man, is eager to lynch Tom from a tree. In the end Tom is killed trying to escape from an imprisonment to which he had been unjustly condemned.

All these experiences, seen through Scout's eyes as a child and related by her when she is a mature woman, dramatically reveal the difference between what she perceived to be true and what is really true. Boo Radley and Mrs. Dubose are eventually recognized by Scout and Jem as good and courageous people. They also realize that the placid surface of Maycomb County conceals racist attitudes that are ugly and, in the case of the innocent Tom Robinson, deadly.

ASSIGNMENT 3

Sometimes teachers will set out the purpose of an essay in the form of a title, a provocative statement, or a quotation, rather than a question. Clarify important instructional terms, such as "analyze," "evaluate," and "discuss" with your teacher before embarking on the assignment. Initially, your teachers will usually provide you with questions to get you started on an essay. But increasingly you will be encouraged to design your own questions to investigate.

To illustrate a different approach, let us assume that your teacher has assigned *Animal Farm* by George Orwell as the topic for an essay of 800 words. You are required to narrow the focus and to formulate your own question. The essay is due in one month's time and some class and homework time will be allocated to the preparation. By now you have shaped a pathway for your writing assignments and because you are aware of the different stages in the process of producing an essay, you can plan a schedule for the completion of the essay on *Animal Farm*.

Your first task is to undertake an exploratory reading of the novel to identify those aspects and features that could provide a challenging focus for an analysis of the text. Remember to isolate the major themes and literary devices as you read. Thoughtful literary analysis (and successful essays) hinge on discovering and then explaining the **relationship between the themes and the use of literary devices.**

Record these ideas in your *I.Q. Journal*. In this instance the teacher has decided to lead a class brainstorming session and compile a list on the chalkboard of all the ideas and suggestions generated by the students during their exploratory reading of *Animal Farm*. Add the new ideas from the brainstorming session to the list in your *I.Q. Journal*.

The next step is to choose **one** aspect on which to focus the essay. Let us assume that you decide to focus on the use of allegory in *Animal Farm*. Whether you are writing a social studies research report or an essay on a literary work, a concise and challenging question is the most effective way of giving direction to your project. After careful thought and consultation with your teacher, you design your question as follows: "How does George Orwell's portrayal of the animals make *Animal Farm* a powerful allegory?"

Since you have already read *Animal Farm* to isolate the major themes, devices, and ideas, you will have a basic understanding of the novel. You can now begin the detailed analysis of the text in response to your question. As you reread the novel, record the information and examples that will help you answer the

question. The preparation or pre-writing process, as outlined below, varies only slightly from the process used in the earlier essays on "Long, Long After School" and *To Kill a Mockingbird*. It is not always possible or necessary to do the preparatory reading in the case of a lengthy literary work, provided that you have read the work **at least once** before you start the detailed analytical reading and notetaking.

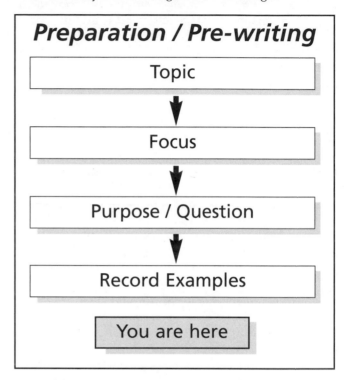

Preparation / Pre-writing

Topic

↓

Focus

↓

Purpose / Question

↓

Record Examples

You are here

Once you have completed analyzing the text and recording the relevant ideas, details, and examples, you can start shaping and composing your answer to the question. As in the earlier essays, your answer or response represents your thesis or point of view — it is **the axis on which the essay revolves.**

The next step is to organize your notes under the Basic and Skeleton outlines to ensure a clearly structured answer. The Basic Outline for the Orwell essay is reproduced below. Since you understand the outlining

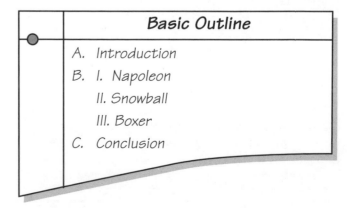

Basic Outline

A. Introduction
B. I. Napoleon
   II. Snowball
   III. Boxer
C. Conclusion

process now, we have not provided the Skeleton Outline. As an exercise, you may wish to "deconstruct" the sample essay and create a Skeleton Outline.

In the earlier essays the teacher set the questions, but you have formulated the question for the essay on *Animal Farm*. Somehow you have to communicate the question or purpose of your essay to the reader. The role of the title is to indicate the focus of the essay — it is not an appropriate place to state the question. How then do you communicate the purpose or objective of the essay to the reader?

The introduction is where the purpose of the essay is explained. In shorter essays on works of literature, where normally only one paragraph is required for the introduction, it is both difficult and awkward to integrate a question in the text of the introduction. Furthermore, many English teachers oppose inserting a question into the introduction.

Introduce the essay by describing the relevant themes and literary devices and their relationship. Then state clearly your response to the question and indicate briefly how you will develop the response. This is known as the **thesis statement** — it is the key element in the introduction. Read the three sample introductions in this chapter on pages 32, 35, and 37 to determine how effectively you think they "introduce" the essays that follow.

The combination of a **precise title** indicating the focus of the essay and a **well-defined thesis statement** in the introduction will usually provide the reader with a clear sense of direction. You must always clarify with your teachers the length, the nature, and the structure of introductions to essays on works of literature. Check also the use of the first person pronoun in the thesis statement. Many teachers discourage the use of the pronoun "I" in an essay.

Set aside time to rough out a draft of the complete essay. With the outlines supplying the paragraph structure and the supporting details, it will be easy to prepare a rough draft. Where the teacher has stated a word length for an essay, for example 800 words, always stay within five percent of the word total stipulated. Since direct quotations play an important role in writing essays on literary works, review pages 31 and 61 on the use of quotations. The parenthetical MLA style has again been used for documenting or citing the quotations from *Animal Farm*.

Fine tune the essay by revising and editing it carefully. Lay it out neatly. Finally, proofread the complete essay eliminating all errors before handing it to your teacher. You will notice that the process for outlining, drafting, and writing the essay on the role of allegory in *Animal Farm* is identical to the method, illustrated on page 32, used in the earlier essays.

Allegory in *Animal Farm*

Aaron Barth
English 2E

Mr. Penton
20 April 2002

In *Animal Farm* George Orwell employs the literary device of allegory to convey the feelings created by a revolution. The setting of a farm represents a nation, and the animals represent the various leaders and groups involved in the revolutionary upheaval. Each animal's character and actions mirror the attitudes and deeds of the participants in a revolution. Napoleon, the leader, behaves in the same heartless manner as the commanders of many uprisings in the past. Snowball, a naive idealist, is exiled by Napoleon, illustrating what happens to those who oppose the views of the ruthlessly ambitious. Boxer, representing the toiling citizens, suffers through the hardships of daily life but receives little credit for his loyalty and tenacity. The portrayal of the characters in *Animal Farm* gives the allegory a powerful authenticity.

After living for generations as slaves under the authority of human beings, the animals of Manor Farm successfully overthrow their oppressors and take control of the farm. The pigs, being the wisest, assume the leadership as a group. However, Napoleon, one of the pigs in power, gains control of the farm by force, using a band of dogs that he has trained. Described as "a fierce-looking boar . . . with a reputation for getting his own way" (9), Napoleon establishes himself as the leader of the new "Animal Farm," and no one is willing to stop him because of the threat posed by his vicious guard dogs. The raising of these dogs in secret by Napoleon strengthens his hold on the farm. When certain pigs try to oppose him, "the dogs round Napoleon let out deep, menacing growls, and the pigs fell silent and sat down again" (37). Napoleon keeps the seven commandments, the rules that were laid down following the revolution. These rules do not permit any of the principles of humanity, such as walking upon two legs, dressing in clothes, and consuming alcohol. However, as time passes, Napoleon modifies each of the commandments. No animal, however, dares to question Napoleon's changes, and as a result he becomes the unchallenged leader of the farm.

Snowball is a pig who has been actively involved in the affairs of Animal Farm. "Snowball was a more vivacious pig than Napoleon, quicker in speech and more inventive, but was not considered to have the same depth of character" (9). Snowball designs many plans for operating the farm. He has high hopes for implementing the revolutionary ideals for which they have fought. He makes "it a point of honour to get in the harvest more quickly than Jones and his men could do" (16). As Napoleon begins to violate the principles of the revolution, he and Snowball start arguing and their relationship deteriorates quickly. Snowball opposes Napoleon over the issue of whether or not to build a windmill to generate electricity. "At this moment Napoleon stood up and . . . uttered a high-pitched whimper . . . and nine enormous dogs . . . dashed straight for Snowball" (35). Snowball is chased off the farm and proclaimed a criminal for opposing Napoleon's will.

Boxer, the strongest horse on the farm, is described as one of the "most faithful disciples" (11). He obeys whatever order he is given without question, and often proclaims: "If Comrade Napoleon says it, it must be right!" (55). He inspires the other animals and encourages perseverance by living up to his motto: "I will work harder!" He supports Napoleon throughout the changes that follow the successful rebellion. He toils at his labours until his lungs collapse and it becomes physically impossible for him to work. Since his productive life is over, Napoleon orders a "veterinarian's" truck to pick Boxer up. The other animals happily bid Boxer a joyous farewell. However, their joy ends abruptly when Benjamin, the donkey, points out the words on the side of the van: *"Alfred Simmonds, Horse Slaughterer and Glue Boiler, Willingdon. Dealer in Hides and Bone-Meal."* "Don't you understand what this means?" cries Benjamin, "they're taking Boxer to the knacker's!" (82).

Orwell uses the three animals to illustrate the roles of a person or group of people involved in a revolution. Napoleon, a rugged pig, is power-driven and, like a boar, desires more and more of the power on which he feeds. Snowball, an imaginative but ingenuous pig, is chased away like many of those who oppose autocratic leaders. Boxer, the horse, like the citizens of many countries, has little choice but to follow the orders of those above him, and in the end receives no recognition for his contributions. The use of animals in *Animal Farm* to symbolize the various participants in a revolution makes the allegory especially powerful because they depict the characters so accurately and vividly.

Work Cited

Orwell, George. *Animal Farm.* London: Penguin, 1951.

As you progress through high school, you will be writing increasingly more complex essays on literary genres, such as poems, plays, short stories, and novels. You will also be exposed to more complex forms, such as commentaries, comparative essays, and research papers. But no matter the genre, the approach, or the format — if you have developed a "process pathway," you will be able to handle any assignment with confidence and success.

An essay is a formal piece of writing with an argument or thesis or point of view. An essay is not a narrative chronicle, an expository report, a biographical account, or a descriptive composition. An essay allows you to develop your own opinion but requires that you support that opinion or point of view with ideas, reasons, and evidence. Unlike the neutral theme of a factual report, an essay has your personal imprint in the form of a thesis or argument — **no argument, no essay.**[3]

To illustrate the difference between a report and an essay, consider an article and an editorial in your student newspaper. An article describing a basketball game would be similar to a report, while an editorial arguing the advantages of compulsory school uniforms would be similar to an essay.

If you are assigned a "term paper" or a "research project," check with your teacher to determine whether it is an essay or a report. Heading off in the wrong direction at the start of your journey could be disastrous.

RESEARCH

Selecting the Topic

Let us assume that your teacher has allowed you to choose the topic for your history essay. It will be a research paper of approximately 1500 words. After careful thought, you select Native North Americans as the broad subject area you wish to investigate. We will use Native North Americans as our topic to illustrate the process for researching and writing a major essay.

Always discuss your choice of topic with your teacher and clarify the following items before you start the research:

- Whether both primary and secondary sources should be used.

- The number of sources required.

- The length of the completed essay.

- The due date and whether there is a late penalty.

- The schedule for different stages, such as finding sources and producing research notes.

- Whether both class and homework time will be allocated to the essay.

- The overall structure, such as the nature of the introduction and the conclusion.

- The use of illustrations.

- The documentation procedures required.

- Whether an oral presentation will also be required.

- The criteria for assessment and whether a sample evaluation form is available.

- The requirements for the final copy.

Although a report and an essay have distinctive features, the process for preparing them is basically the same. Therefore, ensure that you have mastered the process for writing a research report before undertaking a major essay or research paper. Refer to the route map on page 2 when you plan your schedule. Allow equal time for each of the three main phases of the project:

1. The preliminary work up to "Assembling Sources."

2. Recording information and ideas.

3. Outlining, drafting, and preparing the final copy.

Narrowing the Focus

A good essay has depth. You can avoid common problems, such as superficial and vague essays (and reports) by **focusing on one specific issue.** Concentrate on diving for depth and detail like a cormorant or a loon; do not simply paddle around like a duck, contentedly feeding just below the surface.

Some topics may be broad, such as Canadian-American Relations, and require narrowing, while others may be fairly narrow already, such as the Newfoundland Cod Fishery. Let us return to our example, Native North Americans. Like the Great Lakes topic for the report, Native North Americans is too broad and it must be narrowed before you continue your research.

In addition to the approaches suggested earlier on page 4, you can use newspaper and periodical indexes for your exploratory reading. If, for example, you look in *Readers' Guide* under "Indians (Americans)," you will find a lengthy list of features and aspects relating to Native North American societies. Likewise, if you look in the *Canadian Periodical Index* under "Indians of North America," you will find another extensive list. Scan the section headings and the titles for interesting ideas for your project. Check newspaper indexes in the same way. Another approach is to look in the table of contents and indexes of books, such as *Indians of North America*.

Gather a group of students to generate and exchange ideas. Brainstorming in a group is an excellent way of expanding your list of ideas, features, and issues. Just as it was important to involve your group at every stage of preparing the zebra mussel report, so it is important to discuss, cooperate, and share the progress of your essay.

Jot down all the ideas and issues in your *I.Q. Journal*, as shown below. Shape your list of ideas whatever way you please. You will notice that our list is divided into two categories. Alternatively, you may wish to sketch out a "mapping diagram," as illustrated on page 5.

Native North Americans	
Issues:	**Nations:**
Spiritual values	Sioux
Nomadic groups	Huron
Land	Iroquois
Treaties	Plains Indians
Trade	Makah
Agriculture	Cherokee
Hunting	Micmac
Political organization	Beothuk
Reservations	Navajo
European contact	Nishga
Role of women	Cree
Art	Blackfoot
Medicine	Ojibwa
Bison	Haida
Totem poles	Piegan

Since you are preparing an essay with an argument, not an expository report, you should avoid issues that may lead to biographical, narrative, or descriptive treatment. By focusing your essay on **controversial issues and problems,** such as the disappearance of the dinosaurs or the early exploration of North America, you can avoid the biographical and narrative trap.

After considering the list of issues and features in your *I.Q. Journal,* you may decide to focus your research on a specific nation, such as the Huron. Sometimes the narrowing process will involve **two or more stages,** as shown in the "ice cream cone" below. You may decide that the Huron nation is still too broad to investigate and that you need to do further exploratory reading in an encyclopedia or other reference sources. As a result of this reading you discover that the Huron were prominent traders in northeastern North America so you decide to focus on their trading system.

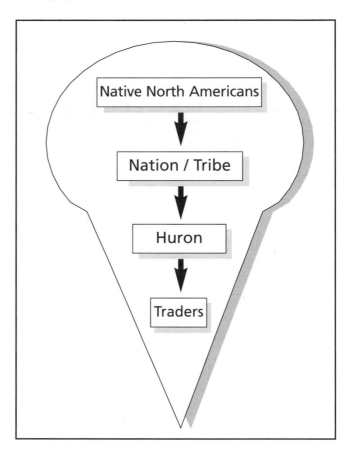

Imagine that your topic is a scene you are viewing through a wide-angle zoom lens.[4] You note all the important features visible in the view finder of the camera. Then you zoom in closer until a specific feature is clearly framed and focused. All your attention will now be concentrated on this feature.

Discuss your choice of focus with your teacher. Remember that it is a good idea to have one or two backup issues on your short list in case you run into difficulties with your first choice. Narrowing the topic and fixing your focus on a specific issue, aspect, problem, or feature is a crucial stage in preparing your essay since **the issue you select becomes the sole focus for the research.** Ensure that the issue you select is manageable, that is neither too big nor too small.

Searching for Sources

You may already have decided on an interesting question to pursue. In that case, simply reverse the next two stages, "Searching for Sources" and "Defining the Purpose." However, if you do not have a research question in mind, start searching for sources on the issue or problem you have selected. Building your Working Bibliography first has certain advantages:

- You will be able to determine quickly whether there is enough potential information on the issue you selected. If not, you can change immediately to one of your backup choices.

- Titles, subtitles, and abstracts of sources can suggest interesting and challenging research questions.

Most of the research tools and techniques that you will need for your school projects were listed on page 6. Some of these you will have used for the research report. Review the list and try some new searching strategies for this project. Always attempt to use a combination of print and electronic resources.

Not many years ago, lack of information for school projects was a common problem for students. Today, the problem is reversed — there is a vast amount of data and students can be overwhelmed by the quantity of information available. Searching on the Internet has been compared to someone trying to sip water from a wide open fire hydrant.

The Internet is not a library; it is more like a gigantic electronic bookstore where not only are the titles listed, but the contents of many documents are also available. However, the sources are not compiled and organized like a library, and, therefore, you may score thousands of "hits," many irrelevant, when doing your research. There are also other limitations, such as copyright, that restrict the availability of quality material on the Internet. Furthermore, access to many of the best databases is limited to those who pay fees. While the Internet does offer free material, much of it is of questionable quality.

Despite these limitations, computers provide distinct advantages for building a comprehensive Working Bibliography. Besides quick access to sources, you can search by keyword or you can link terms to narrow your search. For example, if you are researching Inuit folklore, you can enter "Inuit and folklore" and the search engine will list the sources where both terms appear. Cyberspace is in constant flux and evolution, and consequently it is impossible to provide current and comprehensive details on using the Internet. Search engines and web sites, such as *SearchEngineWatch.com,* have help pages with advice on research methods. Also consult your librarians for advice on the latest searching techniques.

Many databases are also available on CD-ROM and DVD. While not as current as Internet resources, these databases are readily accessible in most libraries at no cost. Furthermore, the contents have usually been evaluated before being selected by experts.

Instead of compiling your Working Bibliography on pages of notepaper or in electronic files, you may want to try index cards this time. One source is entered on each card, as shown on the next page. List all the publication details accurately, especially your Internet sources and their addresses or Universal Resource Locator (URL). You should also bookmark your Internet sources so that you can locate them quickly again. If you prefer to use a computer to build your Working Bibliography, you can adjust the paper type in word processors like *Word* or *WordPerfect* to create your own electronic cards. Alternatively, software designed specifically for creating index cards is also available.

As you search the various resources, both print and electronic, you will be looking for potential sources of information on the issue or problem that is the focus of your research. A format other than APA has been used to enter the details on the bibliographic cards opposite. The format for laying out the final bibliography will be explained later. The code represents a shortened form of the title that will identify the source and speed up the research process.You can

CFN

Dickason, Olive. *Canada's First Nations: A History of Founding Peoples from Earliest Times.* 3rd ed. Toronto: Oxford University Press, 2002.

DS

Archaeological Survey of Canada. *The Draper Site.* 20 July 2001. <http://www. civilization.ca/cmc/archeo/oracles/draper/ drape.htm> [25 July 2002].

WHOS

Castellano, Marlene Brant. "Women in Huron and Ojibwa Societies." *Canadian Woman Studies* 10, no. 2 (1989): 45-48.

CA

Trigger, Bruce. *The Children of Aataentsic: A History of the Huron People to 1660.* Montreal: McGill-Queen's University Press, 1987.

Public Library (Main branch), 970.3

---

discover additional sources by searching under terms related to your issue. For instance, if you are exploring folklore among the Inuit, do not just look under "folklore" and "Inuit." Consider searching under related headings, such as:

- First Nations
- Eskimo
- legends
- fables
- mythology
- traditions
- customs
- oral traditions

You should try to include **primary material** when searching for your sources. Primary material includes the accounts of eyewitnesses, personal memoirs and recollections, literary works, and official documents. Primary sources may be in published form, such as a novel, an autobiography, a journalist's report, or a government document, for example, an international treaty. Primary information is often unpublished, such as taped speeches, letters, and diaries. Original photographs, works of art and films are also regarded as primary material. Primary information is available in statistical form, such as climate data and election details. You can collect your own primary material by interviewing experts and eyewitnesses and by conducting surveys.

Most of your sources will probably be secondary works, such as books, articles, and electronic documents. **Secondary sources** are based on primary material. They are written at a later date and they represent another person's interpretation and explanation of the primary material.

Use your research skills to build a wide-ranging bibliography, covering both primary and secondary information, in which you include books and articles, print and non-print sources, audio-visual and electronic sources, and old and new material. You will notice that our Working Bibliography contains some older works. A recent date of publication does not always indicate a reputable and reliable source.

You may wish to classify your sources in groups to ensure a diversified range of material. You can use different coloured index cards, for example, blue for books and green for Internet documents to distinguish the different categories of sources. You can group your "electronic index cards" in separate files according to source category.

Once you have ten to fifteen sources listed in your Working Bibliography, you are ready to move on to the next stage of the research. However, if there are insufficient sources available, you will have to select another issue from your backup list. Move fast if you have to change — do not delay. Remember to add any ideas that might serve as a challenging research question to your *I.Q. Journal.*

Defining the Purpose

Without a clear sense of direction and purpose, an essay soon resembles an explorer lost in the woods without a compass. You can give a firm sense of direction to your essay by launching it with a precise and challenging **research question.** The question spells out your purpose. Your task is to answer the question. The answer will form your thesis, argument, or point of view.

Since your purpose is to develop an argument or point of view, you should avoid questions that may lead to biographical, narrative, or descriptive answers, such as "Who was Simon Bolivar?" or "How do the Inuit hunt seals?" Also, do not choose "what if" questions, such as "Would the Zulus have won more battles if they had developed firearms?" This type of speculative question cannot be answered by an examination of factual evidence. "Why" questions, such as "Why did war break out in North America in 1812 ?" are effective because they provide a clear sense of purpose and they also lend themselves to coherent, structured answers.

Start then with a single, challenging question, such as "Why did the Beothuks disappear?" to give clarity of focus and purpose to your research. If you have difficulty developing a research question, you may need to do further reading. You can also brainstorm questions with fellow students. Always sketch or jot down any interesting ideas in your *I.Q. Journal*. You may have listed a number of possibilities when you were building your Working Bibliography. Discuss the most appealing questions with your teacher before making your final decision.

Let us return to our example, the Huron. If our interest is in their trade with the early European explorers and settlers, we might state our research question as follows: "Why did the Huron become the dominant fur traders in northeastern North America between 1600–1650?" With the research question precisely phrased, the direction of the essay is clearly mapped out. **Your sole task is to answer the question.**

Some manuals suggest launching the research with a thesis or hypothesis or even an "educated guess" at the answer to the question. This approach might work well in some subjects, such as the sciences, and in assignments based on statistical data. However, this approach does not normally lend itself to the type of evidence used in the humanities. Starting an assignment in the humanities with the answer (thesis, hypothesis, or "educated guess") may be putting the cart before the horse. Initiating your research with an **open-ended research question,** rather than with the answer is usually a more effective approach.

Preparatory Reading

The preparatory reading is an essential part of the invisible underpinnings of the essay. Remember the iceberg. Investing time in reading about the issue on which you are focusing is well worth it because you are "preparing" yourself for an important stage of the research process: recording the evidence needed to develop your argument or thesis. The preparatory reading will provide you with the background knowledge that will help you develop intelligent questions and assist you in deciding what is relevant and reliable in the answers.

Read widely about your issue in reference works, such as encyclopedias and in some of the shorter sources in your Working Bibliography. While you are reading **keep the research question uppermost in your mind.** Although you are not taking detailed notes at this stage, write down any important responses, ideas, and questions in your *I.Q. Journal*.

Unlike a report, an essay does not usually lend itself to a Working Outline. So do not waste time "spinning your wheels" trying to create a Working Outline. The structure will be shaped later in the process. However, if a Working Outline does emerge during the preparatory reading — as often happens with "why" questions — then use it as the framework for your research.

Once you have completed the preparatory reading, you are ready to move on to the major stage of gathering the ideas and evidence that you will need to develop and support your thesis.

Recording Information and Ideas

Armed with a thorough understanding of your issue from the preparatory reading, a wide-ranging Working Bibliography, and a challenging research question, you are now ready to start recording information and ideas from your sources. All this preliminary work is necessary: there are no shortcuts to success.

First, you have to locate and assemble your sources. As you track down a source, note the library and the catalogue number (if you have not done so already) so that you can find the source again easily if necessary. See the bibliographic card on page 47 for an illustration.

Your responsibility is to develop a thoughtful and convincing answer to your research question. Since you cannot remember everything that you read, **a systematic method** for recording your ideas and information is essential. It is worth remembering the Chinese proverb that the palest ink is better than the most retentive memory.

Research involves analyzing, selecting, and recording information and ideas. Analysis means breaking something down into its smaller parts. As you read through your sources, you examine the material carefully, extracting the important ideas and information (the "smaller parts") that are relevant to your question. Once you have selected the relevant details, record them in your notes. **The research question guides your research.** The question directs the analysis, the selection, and the recording of the evidence.

One of the major problems facing researchers is whether their sources are authentic and whether the information is reliable. Approach your material with a critical and skeptical eye — do not accept information blindly. Pose questions, such as the following, as you read:

- How well known is the author?
- Is an article published in a reputable journal?
- Is the information established fact or personal opinion?
- Is the information accurate? Can it be confirmed by another source?
- Is the author's argument fairly presented and accurately documented?
- Is the style of expression correct and formal?
- Is a review of a book or an article available?

Be especially careful in judging your Internet sources. While there are some excellent resources on the Internet, there are also dubious databases and web sites. Unlike a printed source, such as a book, which is expensive to publish, an Internet document can be "published" with relative ease and minimal expense. Many of these documents have short "lives" — they may exist today and be gone tomorrow. Furthermore, the resources on the Internet are not carefully selected by librarians as are resources in a library. Therefore, it is important to evaluate Internet sources and establish their **authenticity and credibility.** You can obtain useful advice on assessing Internet sources by searching online under "evaluating sources."

Use the questions and criteria in the previous column in conjunction with the suggestions below to determine the reliability of your Internet sources.

- Can you find other documents written by the author?
- Is the document "published" by a recognized organization?
- How recently was the document published or updated?
- On what type of site is the document published?
- Are there signs of bias in the document?
- Are there links to other reputable sites?
- Is there a bibliography of reliable sources?

The computer is simply a tool and its effectiveness as a tool is determined by **how you use it.** Examine your Internet information thoroughly, filter the ideas with caution, and do not just mindlessly download data. A careful and critical user of information is always a more credible and respected writer.

There are four main types of notes:

- Direct quotations.
- Paraphrasing ideas and information.
- Summarizing ideas and information.
- Personal insights, comments, and questions.

Reading, analyzing, selecting, and recording the evidence that you will need to develop your point of view or thesis is a major part of preparing a research paper. Allow at least **one third of the time** that you have set aside to produce your paper for this important stage.

You can use notepaper, index cards, or a computer for your research notes. The choice is yours, unless the teacher has stipulated that you should follow a particular method.

Index Card Method

If you were doing the Huron essay, you would take one of your available sources, for example, *The Children of Aataentsic* by Bruce Trigger and start looking specifically for information relevant to the research question. On page 32 there is a reference to the high population density of the Huron settlements. Since populous settlements would facilitate trading, you would record the information on an index card.

You must identify the source of the note in case you need to refer to it for further details. You must also identify the source in case you have to acknowledge it in a reference note in the essay. By acknowledging your sources, you can avoid charges of plagiarism. There is no need to write out all the publication details (author, title, publisher). Simply use the code which stands for a shortened form of the title. For example, *The Children of Aataentsic* becomes CA, as shown on the bibliographic card on page 43. In addition to the source, you must also indicate the page reference for the information. Therefore, CA 32 indicates that the information is from page 32 of *The Children of Aataentsic*, as shown in the example below.

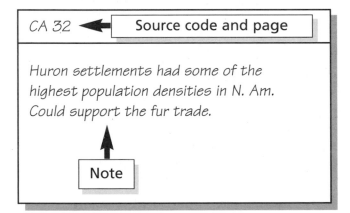

In recording this note, you have:

• Discovered information relevant to the research question.

• Recorded the details in note form.

• Indicated the source and page number.

The **whole process** of analyzing and recording the ideas and evidence needed to develop your thesis is covered in the three steps above. The process is accompanied by continuous probing and questioning as you work your way through the research material.

Continue reading through source CA looking for

information relevant to the research question. On page 34, for example, there is a reference to agriculture providing most of the food supply. Record the information on an index card, as shown, and identify the source and page as explained earlier. Remember to add your own comments in brackets where possible.

CA 35

Crops provided 3/4 of food supply.
(Freed up males to engage in fur trade)

Once you have completed using source CA, check it off as shown on the card on the following page and move on to your next available source. On page 585 of NAI *(The North American Indians)* for example, you find a reference to Huron hospitality. Write down the information verbatim in case it is needed as a quotation. Record it **accurately** and use quotation marks to indicate that it is a quotation. The source code, NAI, and the page reference, 585, are recorded as usual.

NAI 585

Jean de Brebeuf commented: "You can lodge where you please, for this nation above all others is exceedingly hospitable towards all sorts of persons, even towards strangers, and you may remain as long as you please, being always well treated according to the fashion of the country."

Continue reading through source NAI recording information and comments on your cards in the manner described. Use the table of contents and index in each book so that you can save time by reading only the relevant pages.

Read all your available sources searching for ideas and information relevant to the research question and then systematically record the details and identify the sources by code and page on your cards.

Bear these points in mind when you are using index cards for your research:

- Each note card should contain two items:

  1. Source code and page

  2. Note

- Write just one note on each card.

- Use the smallest size index cards. It is easier to shape your outlines later with small cards, each containing just one major point.

- Your research cards have no special order, so do not number them. They are all independent and each one is identified by its source code and page reference.

- Finish writing a long note on the reverse side of the card rather than continuing on another card.

- Paste copies of diagrams, graphs, and statistical tables on your cards.

- Keep separate "date cards" while researching history essays. Creating a chronology or time-line in the appendix will be much easier with "date cards."

- Record your own ideas on separate cards. Use your initials for the source code.

- Do not confuse bibliographic cards, which list sources, with note cards, which contain ideas and information, as shown opposite.

- You can use coloured cards to distinguish different types of cards. For example, you could use white cards for research notes, blue cards for sources, and yellow cards for "date cards." (If you colour coded your Working Bibliography cards as recommended on page 43, then do not use coloured cards as suggested here.)

- Once you have finished using a source to record information, check it off as shown on the bibliographic card in the next column.

- It is a useful practice to make a comment on the reverse side of a bibliographic card about how useful you found the source for your research.

- Use a file box or two-ring card folder to organize your cards.

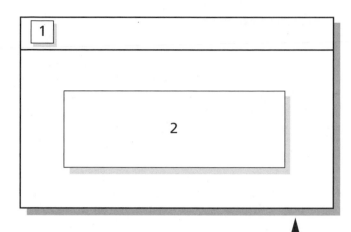

Note (or Information) Card

CA 35

Crops provided 3/4 of food supply.
(Freed up males to engage in fur trade.)

Bibliographic (or Source) Card

CA

Trigger, Bruce. *The Children of Aataensic: A History of the Huron People to 1660.* Montreal: McGill-Queen's University Press, 1987.

✔

Public Library (Main Branch), 970.3

Notepaper Method

Instead of index cards, you can use notepaper to record your information. You will notice a slight difference between the notepaper method used in the zebra mussel report and the method recommended for the Huron essay. The earlier report notepaper system was based on the structure of the Working Outline. When writing essays, however, it is advisable to bypass the Working Outline stage.*

If you have been introduced to writing essays on literary works following the method described in chapter 3, you will find the notepaper method described here virtually identical. The only difference is that because you are using multiple sources for your research essay, you have to insert a code to indicate the source of each note.

Set up your notepaper recording system by ruling a right hand margin of two to three centimetres on the **front side of the page only.** Prepare a number of pages in advance so that you have a supply of notepaper for your research notes.

Take your first source, *The Children of Aataentsic,* and start looking specifically for information relevant to the research question. As you find relevant information, record it in note form in the centre column. Identify the source by its code and give the page reference in the left margin, as shown in the adjacent column.

Work your way through source CA recording relevant ideas and information, as explained. Leave a line between each note so that the notes can be separated later. Nothing is written in the right hand margin. Once you have filled your first page of notepaper, continue on another page. **Do not write on the reverse side** of the page because it will be impossible to separate individual notes later during the outlining process.

Once you have completed using source CA, check it off on your Working Bibliography. Move on to your next available source, *The North American Indians* (coded NAI), and read through recording relevant information in the manner described.

Continue reading all your available sources, searching for ideas and information relevant to your question, and then systematically record the details and identify the sources on pages of notepaper. It is not necessary to start a new page of notepaper for each source provided that you write on one side of the page and you identify the source of each note.

---

* You may set up a Working Outline for your essay if you wish and use the same structured notepaper system described in the report section. See page 50 for instructions.

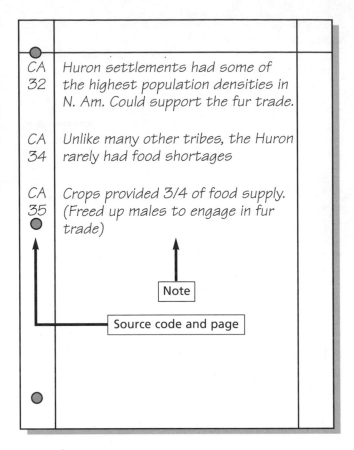

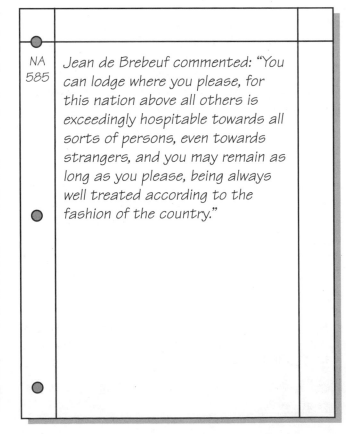

The only difference between the index card and notepaper methods is that the notepaper method links the "index cards" together, as shown below. Later when the notepaper notes are separated, the difference disappears.

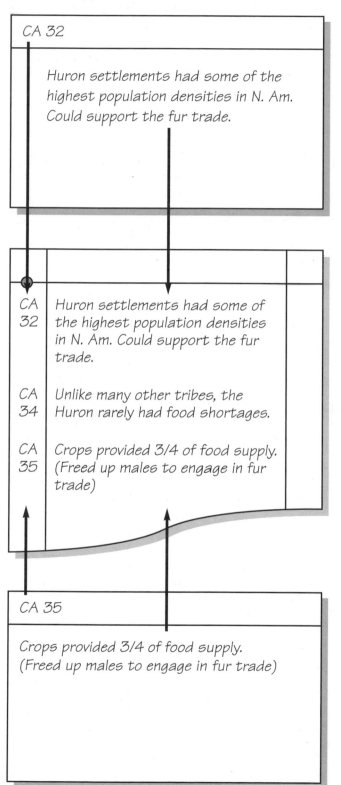

Computer Method

You can also record your ideas and information with a computer. If you prefer using a computer, you should still read pages 46–48 carefully because the notemaking techniques for index cards and notepaper also apply to electronic methods. If you prefer the notepaper procedure, you can set up a file for your notes. If you prefer index cards, there are software packages that will allow you to write, edit, retrieve and sort "cards" on the screen. You can also create your own "electronic cards" using programs like Microsoft *Word* or Corel *WordPerfect*. Record the relevant details, identify the sources, and follow the note procedures just described. Remember to save your material at regular intervals.

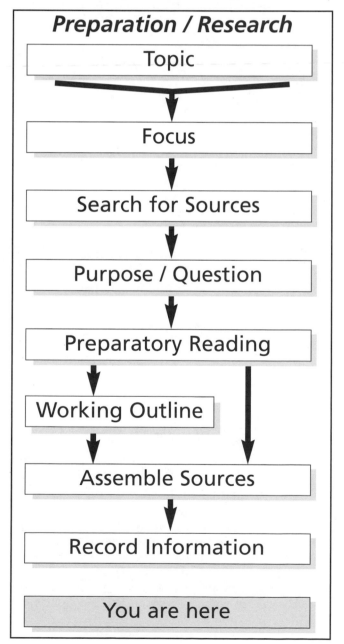

The Working Outline

Some students prefer to structure a Working Outline **before** starting to record their information. If you wish to follow this method, reread page 10 of the report section and then set up a page headed Working Outline in your *I.Q. Journal.* As you do the preparatory reading, keep in mind your research question "Why did the Huron become the dominant fur traders in northeastern North America between 1600–1650?" Then list the main sections (the reasons why the Huron dominated the fur trade) around which you anticipate answering your question, as shown below. **The research question shapes the contents of the Working Outline** — remember the umbilical cord.

Working Outline

A. Introduction

B. Body

    I. Location

    II. Agriculture

    III. People and settlements

    IV. Trading and tradition

C. Conclusion

If you prefer using notepaper for your research, write the sections of your Working Outline at the top of separate pages, as shown on page 11. Then continue to record your information in the same manner as described for the report on pages 11–12.

Another method is to use index cards instead of notepaper. Using index cards **without a Working Outline** was explained on pages 46–47. Read these pages carefully to acquaint yourself with the index card method. The only difference between the two methods is that **with a Working Outline,** you can assign a section number in the top right-hand corner of each card when you write the note. For example, the note card on page 46 would be written as shown below. "III" refers to section B. III of the Working Outline because the information (population density) deals with "People and settlements."

CA 32		III

Huron settlements had some of the highest population densities in N. Am. Could support the fur trade.

If you are using index cards **with a Working Outline,** each card will contain three items:

1. Source code and page

2. Note

3. Section number

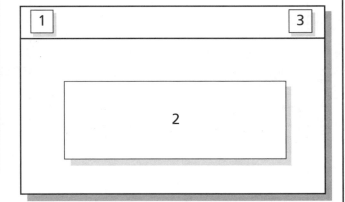

You can also use computer techniques if you decide to pre-structure your research with a Working Outline. Simply set up "notepaper" files or use electronic "index cards" and enter the details, as shown above.

The Working Outline provides a framework for recording information either on notepaper or on index cards. It is not a final plan for the essay because it may change during the research. Your notes (on index cards or notepaper or in an electronic format) will be organized in groups, saving you time when you start shaping your detailed outlines later.

The research process for the report was based on the structure of a Working Outline and on the previous page it was explained how a tentative outline can also supply a framework for the process of researching an essay. However, the advice provided in this manual suggests that the research process for an essay, whether it is on a work of literature or a social studies topic, should not be based on a Working Outline. Essay questions, because they are often more challenging than questions for reports, do not usually lend themselves to a pre-structured outline. The structure will emerge later when you start composing your answer. You will notice from the diagram below that the two research routes — using a Working Outline and bypassing the Working Outline — that forked after the preparatory reading, converge again at the Skeleton Outline stage. The final destination is the same. Once again, the choice of routes is yours.

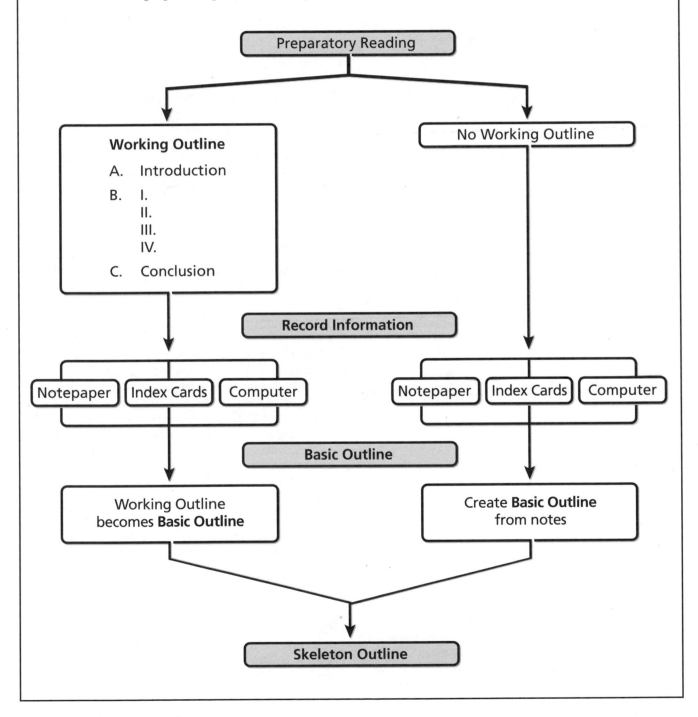

PRESENTATION

Now that the research has been completed, you can start shaping your answer to the question. The research is one side of the coin, the presentation is the other side. The written presentation of an essay is similar to that of a report. The main difference is that the purpose of a report is to inform, explain, or describe, whereas **the purpose of an essay is to present an argument or thesis.** It is your opinion or point of view imprinted on an essay that distinguishes it from other types of writing.

The clarity of your thesis or argument is determined by **the structure and style** of your essay. Contrary to what many people think, structure does not suppress creativity; it promotes clear, creative expression.[5] Once again the ABC formula provides the overall structure for the essay. Style is the mortar or glue that will hold it together.

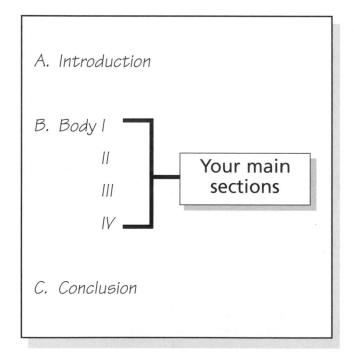

Since we are demonstrating the process of researching an essay **without a Working Outline,** the ideas and information that have been recorded now need to be given structure and order. Once the basic structure of the essay has been established, creating the detailed outlines will be straightforward. And once the outlines have been completed, drafting the essay will be a relatively easy task.

Bias and Subjectivity

Writing essays requires an awareness of the issues of selection, subjectivity, and bias. Selection occurs throughout the process of research and writing. In selecting and narrowing the topic and then deciding on a focus for your research, you had to make choices. You selected certain sources from your Working Bibliography, and then from your reading of these sources you selected your research notes. You have to make further selections from your notes to create your outlines.

Making choices is important when writing essays, which, as has been emphasized, present a personal point of view or argument that is shaped and supported by selected evidence. The questions we ask and the manner in which we select our evidence are influenced by our subjective worldview which in turn is shaped by our upbringing.[6] The tint of the spectacles through which we each view the past and understand the present is forged by our life experiences. Family, friends, and the values of society have all left their imprint. Consider a black student and a white student who grew up under apartheid exploring historical issues in South Africa today. How would a student from an urban ghetto and another from an affluent suburb in a North American city interpret a novel about social class?

We cannot escape our subjective nature but we can be meticulous in the way we evaluate our sources and critical about how we select our supporting evidence. It may be difficult to remain impartial on some contentious issues, but we must strive at all times to be fair and honest researchers and writers. That means we must avoid bias. Bias is a conscious selection of information to present a preconceived point of view.[7] Bias is prejudging an issue, and that is prejudice. **Bias is unacceptable. Subjectivity is unavoidable.**

Since subjectivity shapes selection, you will find differing opinions on many issues among authorities and even among your peers. It is the nature of humanities and social studies research that equally valid views and conclusions can emerge from a single controversial issue. Furthermore, interpretations and theories are not static and conclusive — not even in the sciences is there "final proof." Consider recent opposing theories about global warming. You may find that, after further investigation of an issue, such as the exploration and settlement of North America by indigenous peoples, you change your initial position.

Shaping the Outlines

On completion of your reading and recording, your notes will be on notepaper, index cards, or on computer files. Never attempt to write the final copy straight from your notes. A number of intermediate stages are necessary to complete a successful essay. The next step is to create an outline in which you will organize your notes.*

Basic Outline

Allow time in your schedule to read and reflect on your notes. As you read through your notes, keep the research question uppermost in your mind. Write down the main factors around which you can structure your answer. In the example below, are listed the main factors that will be used to develop an answer to the question: "Why did the Huron become the dominant fur traders in northeastern North America between 1600–1650?" This list of main factors is called the Basic Outline. You must ensure that all sections of the outline **directly address your research question.**

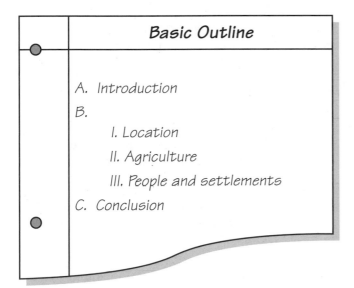

```
                Basic Outline


  A.  Introduction
  B.
          I. Location
          II. Agriculture
          III. People and settlements
  C.  Conclusion
```

There is no magic number of sections in a Basic Outline — from three to six main factors will handle most questions. The basic structure of the essay is now in place, although it is possible that the actual order of the main sections may change during the drafting stage.

---

* If you used a Working Outline for your research, your notes will already be partly organized. Arrange the Basic Outline as explained for the report on page 13.

Go through your note cards and arrange them in groups according to the Basic Outline. If you used notepaper for recording your information, separate the individual notes with scissors (that is why you wrote on one side only) and group the strips according to the Basic Outline.

The next step is to number the cards or notepaper strips according to the section of the Basic Outline into which they fall. Use the upper right-hand corner of the index cards or the right-hand column of the notepaper strips for the numbers, as shown below. For instance, all cards or strips dealing with people and settlements are labeled III because "People and settlements" is section B. III of the Basic Outline shown in the previous column.

```
CA 32                                    III

    Huron settlements had some of the
    highest population densities in N. Am.
    Could support the fur trade.
```

```
CA  | Huron settlements had some of
32  | the  highest population densities |  III
    | in N. Am. Could support the fur
    | trade.
```

Assign section numbers to your electronic cards or notepaper, as described above. You can then group your "cards" according to the Basic Outline by cutting and pasting. If you used the electronic "notepaper" method, you can create separate files for each section of the Basic Outline and transfer the notes to the appropriate files.

Some notes will not fit into the major sections and you will have to put them aside. Do not worry if you cannot use all your notes. To try and force every note into your essay would destroy its clarity. The rejected notes are not wasted; they are part of the "invisible foundations" of the iceberg that will help you develop a clear argument.

Skeleton Outline

Since the Huron essay is a major assignment of approximately 1500 words, the Skeleton Outline plays a slightly different role than earlier in the shorter report and the shorter essays on literary works. The role of the Skeleton Outline in a major assignment is **to provide the substructure** of the major sections, not the supporting details.

Your notes are all grouped and numbered according to the sections of the Basic Outline. The advantage of index cards or notepaper strips is that you can spread them out on a table by sections, thus making it easier to move the cards and strips around and map out the substructure for each section, as shown below.

Your electronic notes are also grouped according to the Basic Outline. It is easy to print the notes and arrange them as described above or view them on the screen and then create the substructure. Most word processing programs have an "Outline" function. This function will help you number the sections and subsections as you shape your outlines.

The introduction is an important part of a major research paper and you will have to shape the substructure of the introduction in the Skeleton Outline. Note below the subsections that are usually part of the introduction to a research paper.

Skeleton Outline

A. Introduction
   1. Background
   2. Focus
   3. Question/Purpose
   4. Thesis
B. I. Location
     1. Trade with North
     2. Trade with French
   II. Agriculture
     1. Surplus and trade
     2. Men freed up
   III. People and settlements
     1. Hospitality
     2. Reliable
     3. Density
C. Conclusion

Point-form Outline

Once you have mapped out the substructure of the Skeleton Outline, you need to isolate the supporting details for your argument. The supporting details are arranged under the overall structure of the Basic and Skeleton outlines, as shown on the opposite page. This stage is known as the Point-form Outline.

Reread your notes carefully selecting only what is reliable, relevant, and **essential** to your argument. Do not try to cram all your notes into the essay because you will overwhelm the reader with unnecessary details and destroy the clarity of your answer. Remember how much of the iceberg is underwater.

Search through your electronic notes looking for the supporting details for the Point-form Outline. Most word processors allow you to split your screen into two windows enabling you to develop your outline in one window while viewing your notes in the other window. Once you have composed your Point-form Outline, print a copy so that you can review and revise it. Remember to save your material as you develop your outlines.

Take care how you select your information, and at all times remember the distinction between bias and subjectivity. To consciously select information to promote a predetermined position is bias — that is unethical in academic research and writing. Keep an open mind and maintain **a fair and balanced approach** in composing your argument.

You should use as few words as possible in your Point-form Outline. It is a waste of time to rewrite your notes. You can always refer to your research notes for additional details when writing the rough draft. Since the order of the main sections of the body may change during the drafting, it is a good idea to use a separate page for each major section in the Point-form Outline, as shown on the opposite page.

Remember that the purpose of your essay is to develop an answer to your research question and to present it in the form of an argument or thesis. You are not simply describing the fur trade in the Huron territory — you are explaining **why** you think the Huron became the dominant fur traders. It is **your point of view** that is stamped on the essay.

Although the Point-form Outline is a new stage in the process, it should neither be a lengthy nor a complex step. The Point-form Outline, containing the supporting details, is simply a further breakdown of the structure of the Basic and Skeleton outlines. Notice at the bottom of the opposite page how "B. III People and settlements" expands at each outline stage.

A. Introduction

1. Background
   - active trade
   - intermediaries
2. Focus
   - Huron fur trade
3. Question/Purpose
   - why dominant traders?
4. Thesis
   - 3 factors

B. II. Agriculture

1. Surplus and trade
   - flourishing crops
   - hunting
   - surplus food to trade
2. Men freed up
   - women managed crops
   - men cleared fields
   - men able to travel
   - Jenness quotation

B. I. Location

1. Trade with North
   - North lacked food
   - had many furs
2. Trade with French
   - access to St. Lawrence
   - rivers as canoe routes
   - knew the land

B. III. People and settlements

1. Hospitality
   - welcomed strangers
   - Brebeuf quotation
2. Reliable
   - large villages
   - permanent structures
   - soil exhaustion
3. Density
   - highest in N.A.
   - support fur trade

Basic	Skeleton	Point-form

B. III. People and settlements	**B. III. People and settlements**
	1. Hospitality
	2. Reliable
	3. Density
		B. III. People and settlements
		1. Hospitality
		  - welcomed strangers
		  - Brebeuf quotation
		2. Reliable
		  - large villages
		  - permanent structures
		  - soil exhaustion
		3. Density
		  - highest in N.A.
		  - support fur trade

The Rough Draft

Once you have completed the Point-form Outline most of the hard work is over. If you arranged the sections of the Point-form Outline on separate pages, it is easy to rearrange them in the most appropriate order. Normally an **ascending order** of interest and importance is the most effective way of developing your thesis.[8] Discuss the order of the sections with your group and your teacher before starting on the rough draft.

Do not attempt to write your final copy straight from the Point-form Outline. Allow time in your schedule so that you can prepare a rough draft first. Roughing the **whole essay** out from title page to bibliography in a preliminary draft and in the required format will both speed up the completion of the final copy and improve it.

Many of the features for presenting an assignment were covered in the report and so only a few more will be added in this section. Check with your teachers again about their preferences and clarify the requirements below before you start your rough draft.

- the length

- the method of documentation

- the use of quotations

- the overall structure

- the use and positioning of illustrations

- the need for an appendix

- style and expression

- the title page

- the table of contents

Once you have finalized the order of the main sections, the shape of your essay will have emerged. You are now ready to weave your essay together. All the work that went into developing the detailed outlines will pay off.

The ability to express your ideas in **clear, correct, concise prose** is of crucial importance. Not only will a competent command of language enhance the clarity of your argument, it will also make it more convincing. Since language and expression are so important in developing your essay, you should reread the section on "Style" (pages 83–86) before you start to prepare your first draft.

The **clarity** of your argument is largely dependent on the **style** of your expression and the **structure** of your answer. The Point-form Outline supplies the structure and the supporting details in a major research paper. It also provides a formula for shaping your paragraphs. Grammatically correct and fluently written paragraphs will bring the structure to life and enhance the clarity of your argument.

Subheadings tend to break up the flow of an essay and fragment the argument. Careful paragraphing eliminates the need for subheadings, because explicit topic sentences provide the signposts that will guide your readers through the essay. Subheadings are more commonly used in major research reports but not usually in essays.

With a detailed structure in place, a clear idea of the direction your essay is taking, a good knowledge of your research notes, an awareness of the importance of style, and a clear grasp of the main features of the essay, writing the rough draft will not be difficult. If you have carefully laid the groundwork and developed a Point-form Outline, writer's block will not be a problem.

Before starting to rough out your draft, check the marking criteria again with your teacher. Remember that it is the **quality** of your project that will determine the result. Only **you** can control the quality.

If you have typed up your Point-form Outline on a computer, it is easy to flesh it out and weave it into the rough draft. Most word processors allow you to split the screen into two windows and work on two documents at the same time. You could, using this feature, bring up your outline in one window and then begin writing the essay in the other window, as shown below. Alternatively, you could print a copy of your Point-form Outline, place it in front of you and then type up your rough draft on the computer.

You could split the screen and bring up your "electronic notes" in one window and then copy and paste directly into the other window containing your rough draft. This is a feature to be used sparingly since an essay constructed by simply stringing together your research notes will not make any sense to your readers. A better approach would be to work on your rough draft in full screen mode and then pull up the files with your "electronic notes" if you need to copy something directly. You can copy the pertinent information from your research notes, minimize the window until you need it again and then paste the quotation into your rough draft.

Using a computer to prepare your rough draft has many advantages. It will enable you to produce the final copy quickly and efficiently. Most word processors have a feature that will count the number of words in your essay making it easier to ensure that your essay adheres to the stipulated word length. You may even find it useful to increase the line spacing and widen the margins when printing a draft copy so that you will have more white space for revising and editing which you can then remove before printing the final copy. A printed copy will also provide a back-up if you run into technical difficulties. Finally, save your draft at regular intervals to avoid losing all your hard work in the event of a power failure or a computer malfunction.

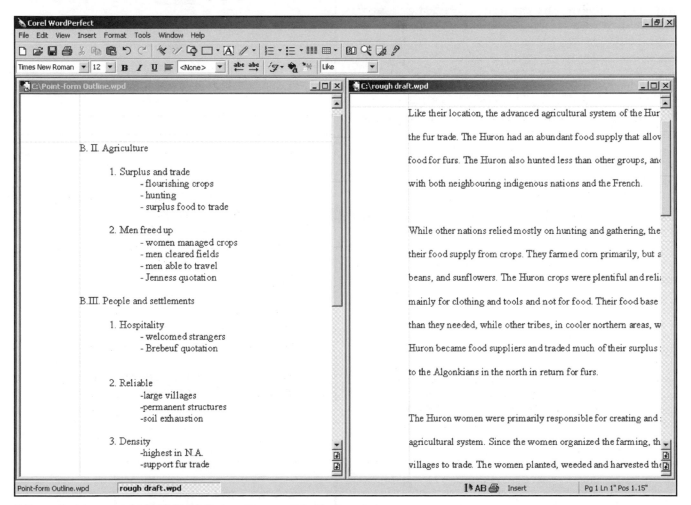

© Screenshot is copyright 2000 Corel Corporation, reprinted by permission.

Drafting the Introduction

The introduction to an essay is short but important because first impressions can influence a reader. Introductions will vary in length between ten and fifteen percent of the overall length of the essay. The length will be determined by the nature of the essay — a controversial issue will probably need a longer introduction — or by the preference of your teacher. But do not allow the introduction to dominate the essay and overshadow the development of your thesis.

If you have followed a systematic research and outlining process, you should have no difficulty in drafting the introduction first. There is no need to leave the introduction until last — almost as an afterthought. Essays and research papers are formal studies so do not try to "grab" the reader's attention by forcing humour or sensationalism into the introduction.

The funnel diagram opposite offers an effective framework for the introduction to a research essay.[9] First you provide any **background** information that your reader needs to know about the topic. Next explain the **focus** of your assignment. Then you should articulate the **purpose** of your essay to indicate the direction it will take. Stating the research question is probably the clearest means of expressing the purpose of the essay. If you find it difficult to integrate a question smoothly in the introduction, try stating the aim of the assignment in a more traditional way, such as "The purpose of this essay is to explain why the Huron dominated the fur trade in northeastern North America between 1600–1650."

Finally, state **your thesis** or argument clearly. Your thesis statement is your answer to the research question summed up in one or two sentences. It is important to inform your readers of your position or argument before you start developing it in the body of the essay. Essays are not detective thrillers where you keep your readers in suspense until the last paragraph.

Another advantage of the funnel formula is that it provides a structure for paragraphing your introduction. In shorter introductions, such as the Huron example opposite, you will probably only need two paragraphs. But in longer introductions a separate paragraph would probably be devoted to each section, as shown in the dinosaur example on the next page.

The introduction to the Huron essay is shown opposite. It follows closely the structure of the funnel formula. Discuss the introduction with your teacher because teachers differ over the contents of an introduction. Some teachers, for example, prefer shorter introductions. Also, while some teachers like the use of "I" in the thesis statement, others discourage using the first person pronoun in an essay.

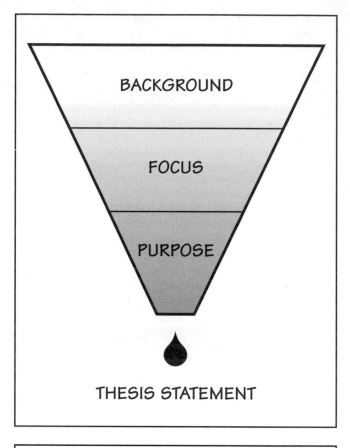

In the seventeenth century, there was an active fur trade between the Natives of North America and the Europeans. From the early 1600's to mid century, the Huron were the most successful traders in a large fur trading empire in the northeastern part of the continent. They were the intermediaries between the Native fur producers in the north and the French explorers and settlers based on the St. Lawrence river. There were many indigenous nations in the region, but the Huron were the dominant traders. This raises the question: Why did the Huron dominate the fur trade in northeastern North America between 1600–1650?

Three factors contributed to the Huron domination of the fur trade. They had a solid agricultural base and they had a favourable location. Also, the French chose to deal with the Huron because they lived in established settlements and welcomed visitors .

Some essays focus on controversial issues, such as the factors surrounding the outbreak of the First World War (1914-1918) or the disappearance of the dinosaurs. If you are writing a major paper on a controversial issue, you might want to add another section to your introduction. To emphasize the attention that your issue has attracted among researchers and writers, you could mention the **different theories, arguments, and interpretations** that it has generated. By referring to the debate surrounding the focus of your essay, you are also indicating its importance as a field of study.

If you include in your introduction the range of interpretations surrounding your issue, then the "funnel" becomes a "coffee filter," as shown below. The other sections of the introduction remain unchanged. The sample introduction to an essay on the dinosaurs opposite illustrates the coffee filter structure.

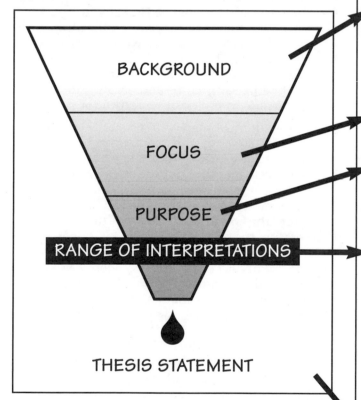

Notice how the components of the coffee filter, which are simply the subsections of the Skeleton Outline, have shaped the paragraph structure for the sample introduction to a major research paper on the controversial issue of the disappearance of the dinosaurs.

Even if you wish to modify these suggestions, strive to write interesting and effective introductions to your essays. No matter the length or the nature of the introduction, remember to mention the **three P's** — the **problem** (or focus), the **purpose** (or question), and your **point of view** (or thesis).

Two hundred million years ago the climate, vegetation, and landscape of North America was quite different when compared with today's geography. The Rocky Mountains had not yet been formed, allowing moist air to flow far inland from the Pacific. Warm seas covered parts of the continent and tropical jungles flourished. This landscape was populated by many species of reptiles, known collectively as dinosaurs. The largest lived on land, others adapted to water, while some were able to fly. The dinosaurs dominated the planet during the Mesozoic era, and then mysteriously disappeared about sixty-five million years ago.

The extinction of the dinosaurs is one of nature's great mysteries. Interest in the disappearance of the dinosaurs has been rekindled in recent years by geological discoveries, technological developments, such as radiometric dating, and by new theories in physics.

The purpose of this essay is to investigate the extinction of the dinosaurs and to explain why they disappeared.

The disappearance of the dinosaurs is a controversial issue. The various theories fall into two main groups: those which argue that extinction was a slow evolutionary process and those which contend that it was a rapid destruction caused by a major catastrophe. The "evolutionary" theories include changes caused by a reversal of the earth's magnetic field, tectonic plate movements, competition from other species, new diseases produced by migrations, and climate and vegetation changes that caused starvation. The "catastrophe" theories centre on either the devastation caused by massive volcanic eruptions or by a collision with an extra-terrestrial object.

The disappearance of the dinosaurs can be attributed to a collision between an asteroid and the earth that caused widespread devastation at the end of the Cretaceous period. It was a single, catastrophic event, not a slow evolutionary process that caused the extinction of the dinosaurs.

Drafting the Body

The body is the most important section of the essay. It is in the body that you develop and substantiate the thesis or argument that you stated at the end of the introduction — **that is the sole function of the body of an essay.** Check carefully that all the ideas and evidence are closely linked to your argument. Irrelevant information will destroy the clarity of your essay and weaken the argument.

With a completed Point-form Outline, it is an easy task to draft the body. In a major essay, it is the Skeleton Outline that provides the paragraph structure while the Point-form Outline supplies the supporting details. Paragraphs are like links in a chain. Just as a chain is only as strong as its weakest link, so your essay is only as effective as its weakest paragraph.

One section of the body has been reproduced to demonstrate how the outlines provide a formula for shaping the paragraphs. Notice how each major section in the Huron example, unlike the shorter report and the literary essays, will have both an introductory paragraph and a concluding paragraph. Note also how the introductory paragraph in the example opposite acts as a transitional paragraph by providing a link with the previous section ("their location").

Paragraphs reflect the structure of your essay and structure is a key component of clarity. **Only you** can establish the ideal number of paragraphs around which to organize your essay. Every essay is unique and the paragraph structure will be shaped by your question, your research, your thinking, and your outlines.

B. II. Agriculture	**(introductory paragraph)**
1. Surplus and trade - flourishing crops - hunting - surplus food to trade	**(paragraph)**
2. Men freed up - women managed crops - men cleared fields - men able to travel - Jenness quotation	**(paragraph)**
	(concluding paragraph)

Like their location, the advanced agricultural system of the Huron was important in supporting the fur trade. The Huron had an abundant food supply that allowed them to trade their surplus food for furs. The Huron also hunted less than other groups, and so the men were free to trade with both neighbouring indigenous nations and the French.

While other nations relied mostly on hunting and gathering, the Huron obtained three-quarters of their food supply from crops. They farmed corn primarily, but also cultivated squash, tobacco, beans, and sunflowers. The Huron crops were plentiful and reliable. In fact, the Huron hunted mainly for clothing and tools and not for food. Their food base left the Huron with more food than they needed, while other tribes, in cooler northern areas, were frequently short of food. The Huron became food suppliers and traded much of their surplus food, especially corn and beans, to the Algonkians in the north in return for furs.

The Huron women were primarily responsible for creating and maintaining a flourishing agricultural system. Since the women organized the farming, the men were able to leave the villages to trade. The women planted, weeded and harvested the crops after the men had cleared the fields. Because the Huron were settled, clearing fields had to be done only infrequently, approximately every ten to twenty years. During the summer, the men were free to travel and trade with the French and with other nations. Historian Diamond Jenness noted that "as soon as the planting ended . . . the men scattered in all directions to trade with neighbouring peoples." In nomadic nations that relied more upon hunting for their food, the men were occupied with hunting in the summer and were unable to trade. The more settled Huron had a major advantage over their neighbours.

The productive agricultural system of the Huron, operated by the women, freed the men up to travel and trade. Less hunting also meant more time to trade. In a profitable exchange network, the Huron traded their surplus food to northern nations for furs and then traded the furs to the French.

Drafting the Conclusion

The conclusion is short, about ten percent of the essay, and usually comprises just one paragraph. However, the conclusion is important because it is your last chance to convince the reader of the validity of your thesis and it provides a sense of closure to the essay. In this section you weave together the main reasons supporting the conclusions that you developed in the body of the essay and you also sum up your arguments.

Sometimes it can be effective to start the conclusion with the research question, since this reminds the reader of the purpose of the essay. But try to be more original than concluding your essay as follows: "In conclusion, I would like to repeat that the dinosaurs disappeared because of disease."

Do not add new information in support of your thesis in the concluding paragraph because it will continue the argument and confuse your readers. All important ideas and information should be included in the body. Also, ensure that any quotations have a specific function and are not simply inserted in the conclusion for purely dramatic effect.

Like the initial impact of the introduction to the essay, **the final impression created by the conclusion is important.** The concluding section of the Huron essay is reproduced here as an example. It is shown in its final format after revising and editing.

> A combination of factors shaped the Huron domination of the fur trade in northeastern North America. The Huron were located between the Native fur producers of the north and the European fur consumers of the south, making them natural trading intermediaries. They had a flourishing agricultural system organized by the women, so that they could support themselves and trade surplus food to other communities. Their productive agricultural base also allowed the men to travel widely and to engage in trade. The Huron relationship with the French was crucial to their trading dominance in the region. The French liked dealing with the Huron because of their hospitality, and the fact that they lived in large, settled communities made them reliable traders. Furthermore, French soldiers provided protection against rivals, such as the Iroquois. The Huron were able to develop and maintain their large trading network because of these advantages over other indigenous nations.

Quotations

Carefully selected quotations can be effective in supporting your arguments. Keep your quotations brief and do not overuse them. It is **your** ideas that the teacher wants to read. Quotations must be firmly anchored in the text of your essay and clearly linked to your thesis.

Short quotations of less than forty words should be included within the text of the essay and placed in double quotation marks. Try to weave the quoted material naturally into your writing.

Historian Diamond Jenness noted that "as soon as the planting ended . . . the men scattered in all directions to trade with neighbouring peoples."

"Gobies are becoming little poison pills," claims biologist Jeff Robinson.

Miss Tretheway pointed out to Marilyn that "Wes's hands are much cleaner than yours. Maybe Wes doesn't like to get his hands dirty."

The narrator's flowers may seem more appropriate than Wes's small corsage "such as a young boy sends his girl for her first formal dance."

Sometimes you may only need to use part of a quotation. Use three spaced periods (. . .) to indicate the missing words. This is known as an **ellipsis.** Any omission of words must not alter the meaning of the quoted passage.

Longer quotations of more than forty words or two or more sentences should be separated from the text, as shown below. Longer quotations are also known as block quotations. The quoted passage is indented five spaces from the left margin. Block quotations are introduced with a colon and they are usually single-spaced and quotation marks are omitted.

Jean de Brebeuf, who had many dealings with the Huron, commented on their hospitality:

> **You can lodge where you please, for this nation above all others is exceedingly hospitable towards all sorts of persons, even toward strangers; and you may remain as long as you please, being always well treated according to the fashion of the country.**

You must quote your material **accurately.** You must also acknowledge your quotations carefully to avoid accusations of plagiarism. The procedures for acknowledging your sources are explained in the next section.

Citing Sources

Whether you are using direct quotations or paraphrased ideas, **you must acknowledge the sources.** Providing the sources of your information gives credit to other writers for their ideas. It also means the information can be checked for accuracy and readers are guided to additional sources of reliable information. Information that is common knowledge does not have to be cited. For example, you do not have to cite the fact that William Shakespeare was born in Stratford- upon-Avon.

Techniques for acknowledging and listing sources are a key element of scholarly writing. It is important that you understand them and learn to apply the different documentation styles during your school career. Although documentation procedures may appear complex initially, you will be surprised at how quickly you will master them with practice.

You were introduced to the APA parenthetical procedure for citing your sources in the presentation of a written report. Another common method for citing your sources is to use numbered footnotes or endnotes. A number is placed above the line at the end of the sentence or quotation. These superscript references are numbered sequentially throughout the essay. Each of these numbers has a corresponding entry either at the bottom of the page (footnote) or on a separate page at the end of the essay (endnote).

The numbered note system is less intrusive than the parenthetical procedure and creates less interruption in the reader's flow of thought. It is a system that is widely used in many subjects, including history. On page 65 we have reproduced sections of the Huron essay to illustrate the use of both footnotes and endnotes. Refer to page 121 to see how endnotes are used in this manual. Word processing programs have footnote and endnote features that will automatically set up your citation notes.

How many citations should there be in an essay is a common question. There is no magic number. The number of your citations will be determined by the nature of your supporting evidence — whether it is controversial or common knowledge, whether the ideas are original, or by the number of direct quotations. Your judgement in using citations, whether they are parenthetical or numbered notes, will improve with experience.

Examples of the more common types of citation or documentary notes follow. They are based on the procedures in Kate Turabian's *A Manual for Writers,* which in turn follows *The Chicago Manual of Style.* All titles have been italicized in these examples. If you are using a word processor, titles should be italicized. In handwritten or typed essays, titles are underlined.

Book

One Author

[1]Nancy Bonvillain, *The Huron* (New York: Chelsea House, 1989), 61.

Two Authors

[2]William Strunk, Jr. and E.B. White, *The Elements of Style* (New York: Macmillan, 1979), 7.

Multiple Authors

[3]Theodora Colborn et al., *Great Lakes, Great Legacy?* (Washington: The Conservation Foundation, 1990), 10.

Editor

[4]Anne Krueger, ed., *The WTO as an International Organization* (Chicago: University of Chicago Press, 1998), 98.

No Author

[5]*The Great Lakes: An Environmental Atlas and Resource Book* (Chicago: United States Environmental Protection Agency and Toronto: Environment Canada, 1995), 21.

Corporate Author

[6]American Psychological Association, *Publication Manual,* 5th ed. (Washington, DC: American Psychological Association, 2001), 201.

Later Edition

[7]William Zinsser, *On Writing Well,* 6th ed. (New York: HarperCollins, 1998), 88.

Magazine

[8]Stephen Leahy, "Lake Erie's small but toxic killers," *Maclean's,* 16 December 2001, 114.

Journal

[9]G.Zorpette, "Mussel Mayhem," *Scientific American* 275 (August 1996): 22-23.

Newspaper

[10]David Binder, "Great Lakes face endless battle with marine invaders," *New York Times,* 11 July 2000, F4.

Encyclopedia

[11]P.Iverson, "Navajo," in *Encyclopedia Americana*, vol. 20 (Danbury, CT: Grolier, 2000), 3.

Yearbook

[12]Michael Yapko, "Repressed Memories: Special Report." *Britannica Book of the Year 1995* (Chicago: Encyclopedia Britannica, 1996), 201.

Videocassette

[13]*The Civil War,* dir. Ken Burns, PBS, 1994, videocassette.

Government Report

[14]International Joint Commission, *Protection of the Waters of the Great Lakes* (Ottawa, ON and Washington, DC: International Joint Commission, 2000), 17.

Interview

[15]Simon Smales, interview by author, 5 June 2000, Toronto, tape recording.

Film

[16]*Dances with Wolves,* dir. Kevin Costner, TIG and Orion, Los Angeles,1990, film.

Radio and Television Program

[17]*The Great Egyptians,* prod. P. Spry-Leverton, narr. B. Brier, The Learning Channel, 27 August 1998, television.

Art

[18]Pablo Picasso, *Still Life with Chair-Caning,* oil on canvas, 1912, Musee Picasso, Paris.

Map

[19]*Physical United States* (Washington, DC: National Geographic, 2000), map.

CD-ROM / DVD

[20]"Sustainability in Lake Ontario," *Discover the Great Lakes: The Ecosystem of the Great Lakes-St. Lawrence* (Ottawa: Environment Canada, 1997), CD-ROM.

Online Sources

Like print or video sources used in a report or an essay, online material must also be documented. Sources of electronic information differ considerably from traditional print sources as explained on pages 42 and 45. Some of these differences directly influence how you cite and list your sources.

Another characteristic of online sources that creates difficulties, both for research and for documentation, is the fleeting nature and ease of alteration of the sources. A source might exist today and disappear tomorrow. Sources are frequently updated and they can be easily modified by deleting or adding details. Furthermore, the URL may change. Since online sources frequently disappear or change drastically, you may wish to print copies or alternatively save them to disk as confirmation of their existence. In the case of lengthy documents, consider printing just the first page.

Besides the fleeting nature of online sources, other differences exist between traditional sources and electronic material. In printed sources, such as a book, a page reference in a citation note indicates the specific location of important material used in the essay. But in electronic documents, page references are seldom used. If possible, try to identify the exact location using either a section heading, a chapter or a paragraph number if a page reference is not provided. This problem is not peculiar to electronic material because sources, such as speeches, films, and interviews do not use page numbers either.

It is necessary to provide two dates when documenting online sources — first the date of publication or latest revision and then the access date that you consulted the source. These two dates are both necessary because of the changing nature of online sources. Accuracy of URL details is critical for online documentation because a missing letter or punctuation mark may prevent a reader from accessing a website. When entering URLs, always enclose them in angle brackets (< >). URLs can be lengthy and it is often necessary to continue on a second line. In such a case, break the URL after a punctuation mark, such as a slash or a period.[10] **Do not hyphenate any split words.**

The examples of citing and listing your online sources shown on pages 64 and 68 are based on the principles of the Chicago/Turabian style. As explained earlier, this style of documentation consists of two components: a numbered footnote or endnote citing the precise reference for the information and a bibliography listing details of the sources. The same source types were used to illustrate APA procedures on page 21 if you wish to draw comparisons between the two styles.

Art

[1]Leonardo da Vinci, *The Mona Lisa* (1506). <http://www.louvre.fr/anglais/collec/peint/inv0779/peint_f.htm> [1 December 2002].

Book

[2]Charles Dickens, *Great Expectations* (1861), 36. <http://www.bibliomania.com/0/0/19/frameset.html> [29 November 2002].

Email

[3]Judy Sandler <judy@example.com> "Re: Zebra mussels" [Email to Susan Conway <sconway@example.com>] (6 July 2002).

Encyclopedia

[4]D.M.L. Farr, "The Alaska Boundary Dispute," *The Canadian Encyclopedia* (2002), par. 4. <http://www.thecanadianencyclopedia.com/index.cfm> Search: "Alaska Boundary Dispute" [25 October 2002].

General Website

[5]Archaeological Survey of Canada, *The Draper Site* (20 July 2001), par. 6. <http://www.civilization. ca/cmc/archeo/oracles/draper/drape.htm> [10 September 2002].

Journal

[6]David Menichetti, "German Policy in Occupied Belgium, 1914-1918," *Essays in History* 39 (1997): Conclusion.<http://etext.lib.virginia.edu/journals/EH/EH39/menich39.html> [9 February 2002].

Magazine

[7]Guy Tal, "Learning to Photograph the Landscape," *Nature Photographers Online Magazine,* (September 2002), par.3. <http://www.naturephotographers.net/articles0902/gt0902-1.html> [27 November 2002].

Map

[8]*The Axis Powers,* 1942, (n.d.). Map. <http://www.indstate.edu/gga/gga_cart/78927.jpg> [13 September 2002].

Newspaper

[9]Steve Schmadeke, "Fierce flies are deployed to fight Florida fire ants," *Naples Daily News* (27 November 2002), par.3. <http://www.naplesnews.com/02/11/naples/d865261a.htm> [1 December 2002].

Photograph

[10]Simon Wiesenthal Center, *Neville Chamberlain with Adolf Hitler* (1997). Photograph. <http://motlc. wiesenthal.com/gallery/pg18/pg7/pg18722.html> [22 June 2002].

Professional Website

[11]Maurice Crouse, *Citing Electronic Information in History Papers* (18 October 2002), Introduction. <http://www.people.memphis.edu/~mcrouse/elcite.html> [18 December 2002].

Question and Answer Database

[12]The Chicago Manual of Style, *FAQ (and not so FAQ)* (2002). <http://www.press.uchicago.edu/Misc/ Chicago/cmosfaq/> [6 December 2002].

Radio / Television

[13]Mark O'Neill, "Chinese Traditional Medicines," *Quirks and Quarks* (23 May 1998). <http://www.radio.cbc. ca/programs/quirks/realaud/may2398.ra> [5 January 2001].

Subscription Database

[14]George Woodcock, "The Secrets of Her Success," *Quill & Quire* 60 (August 1994): 25. *Literature Resource Center.* <http://galenet.galegroup.com/servlet/LitRC> Ottawa Public Library. [2 August 2002].

Footnotes

Reproduced below is a page from the Huron essay, illustrating the use of footnotes.

3.

While other nations relied mostly on hunting and gathering, the Huron obtained three-quarters of their food supply from crops. They farmed corn primarily, but also cultivated squash, tobacco, beans, and sunflowers. The Huron crops were plentiful and reliable.[4] In fact, the Huron hunted mainly for clothing and tools and not for food.[5] Their food base left the Huron with more food than they needed, while other tribes, in cooler northern areas, were frequently short of food. The Huron became food suppliers and traded much of their surplus food, especially corn and beans, to the Algonkians in the north in return for furs.[6]

The Huron women were primarily responsible for creating and maintaining a flourishing agricultural system. Since the women organized the farming, the men were able to leave the villages to trade. The women planted, weeded and harvested the crops after the men had cleared the fields. Because the Huron were settled, clearing fields had to be done only infrequently, approximately every ten to twenty years. During the summer, the men were free to travel and trade with the French and with other nations. Historian Diamond Jenness noted that "as soon as the planting ended . . . the men scattered in all directions to trade with neighbouring peoples."[7] In nomadic nations that relied more upon hunting for their food, the men were occupied with hunting in the summer and were unable to trade. The Huron, living in semi-permanent settlements, had a major advantage.

---

[4]Diamond Jenness, *The Indians of Canada,* 7th ed. (Toronto: University of Toronto Press, 1977), 202.

[5]Bruce Trigger, *The Children of Aataentsic: A History of the Huron People to 1660* (Montreal: McGill-Queen's, 1987), 34.

[6]Nancy Bonvillain, *The Huron* (New York: Chelsea House, 1989), 48.

[7]Jenness, 113.

Endnotes

If you were using endnotes instead of footnotes for the Huron essay, they would be set up as follows.

Notes

1. Olive Dickason, *Canada's First Nations: A History of Founding Peoples from Earliest Times,* 3rd ed. (Toronto: Oxford University Press, 2002),101.

2. Archaeological Survey of Canada, *The Draper Site* (20 July 2001), par. 5. <http://www.civilization.ca/cmc/archeo/oracles/draper/drape.htm> [25 July 2002].

3. Bruce Trigger, *Natives and Newcomers: Canada's "Heroic Age" Reconsidered* (Montreal: McGill-Queen's University Press, 1985), 51.

4. Diamond Jenness, *The Indians of Canada,* 7th ed. (Toronto: University of Toronto Press, 1977), 202.

5. Bruce Trigger, *The Children of Aataentsic: A History of the Huron People to 1660* (Montreal: McGill-Queen's University Press, 1987), 34.

6. Nancy Bonvillain, *The Huron* (New York: Chelsea House, 1989), 48.

7. Jenness, 113.

8. Trigger, *Children of Aataentsic,* 40.

9. Trigger, *Natives and Newcomers,* 99.

10. Dickason, 104.

11. Draper, par. 10.

Endnotes are placed on a separate page just before the bibliography. Head the page "Notes" and enter the details as shown above. Superscript numbers are used in the text and in footnotes (see the previous column) but they are not used in endnotes. Type the number on the line followed by a period and a space, and then enter the citation details as illustrated above. For a further example of the use of endnotes, see page 121 in this manual.

If you refer to a source that has already been cited, there is no need to repeat all the publication details. Just use an abbreviated form containing the author's surname and the page reference, as shown in the Jenness and Dickason examples on this page. In the case of a repeat citation from an author who has two or more works listed in the bibliography, you must identify the specific work each time. Provide the author's last name, a shortened version of the title, and the page reference. Refer to the citations for Bruce Trigger above as an illustration of this procedure.

Listing Sources

As a general rule when using the footnote/endnote documentation method, it is customary to list **all** the sources (not just cited sources) that proved useful in preparing the essay. The sources should be listed in alphabetical order by author's last name on a separate page at the end of the essay. If you used index cards for your Working Bibliography, it is easy to rearrange them in alphabetical order. Any one of the following headings may be used:

- References
- Bibliography
- Sources
- Works Consulted

There is no need for you to group your sources under headings, such as "Books" and "Articles," as recommended for the Working Bibliography. That division was suggested to encourage you to diversify the range of your sources. Your final list of sources should be a **single list** of sources. Do not number each source. See the sample Huron Bibliography on the opposite page and the Works Consulted at the end of the manual for examples of how to list your sources.

The details in a **citation note** and a **bibliographic entry** are usually identical, except for inserting a page reference in the citation note. However, there are slight differences in the format for citing your sources in footnotes or endnotes and listing your sources in the bibliography, as illustrated below.

- Order of names is reversed.
- Punctuation is different.
- Indention is reversed.

Footnotes/Endnotes

[1]Bruce Trigger, *The Children of Aataentsic: A History of the Huron People to 1660* (Montreal: McGill-Queen's, 1987), 335.

Bibliography

Trigger, Bruce. *The Children of Aataentsic: A History of the Huron People to 1660.* Montreal: McGill-Queen's, 1987.

The more common types of sources are listed in the next two columns, followed by online sources on page 68. Once again the sample entries are based on the Chicago/Turabian procedures. If there is no place of publication given, use "N.p." and for no publisher, use "n.p." If both are missing, it is permissible to use just "N.p." If no date is provided, insert "n.d."

Book

One Author

Bonvillain, Nancy. *The Huron.* New York: Chelsea House, 1989.

Two Authors

Strunk, W., Jr., and E.B. White. *The Elements of Style.* New York: Macmillan, 1979.

Multiple Authors

Colborn, Theodora et al. *Great Lakes, Great Legacy?* Washington: The Conservation Foundation, 1990.

Editor

Krueger, Anne, ed. *The WTO as an International Organization.* Chicago: University of Chicago Press, 1998.

No Author

The Great Lakes: An Environmental Atlas and Resource Book. Chicago: United States Environmental Protection Agency and Toronto: Environment Canada, 1995.

Corporate Author

American Psychological Association. *Publication Manual.* 5th ed. Washington, DC: American Psychological Association, 2001.

Later Edition

Zinsser, William. *On Writing Well.* 6th ed. New York: HarperCollins, 1998.

Magazine

Leahy, Stephen. "Lake Erie's small but toxic killers." *Maclean's,* 16 December 2001, 114.

Journal

Zorpette, G. "Mussel Mayhem." *Scientific American* 275 (August 1996): 22-23.

Newspaper

Binder, David. "Great Lakes face endless battle with marine invaders." *New York Times,* 11 July 2000, F4.

Encyclopedia

Iverson, P. "Navajo." In *Encyclopedia Americana*. Vol. 20. Danbury, CT: Grolier, 2000.

Yearbook

Yapko, Michael, D. "Repressed Memories: Special Report." *Britannica Book of the Year 1995*. Chicago: Encyclopedia Britannica, 1996.

Video recording

The Civil War. Directed by Ken Burns. PBS, 1994. Videocassette.

Government Report

International Joint Commission. *Protection of the Waters of the Great Lakes*. Ottawa, ON and Washington, DC: International Joint Commission, 2000.

Interview

Smales, Simon. Interview by author, 5 June 2000, Toronto. Tape recording.

Film

Dances with Wolves. Directed by Kevin Costner. TIG and Orion, Los Angeles,1990. Film.

Radio and Television Program

The Great Egyptians. Produced by P. Spry-Leverton. Narrated by B. Brier. The Learning Channel, 27 August, 1998. Television.

Art

Picasso, Pablo. *Still Life with Chair-Caning*. Oil on canvas. 1912. Musee Picasso, Paris.

Map

Physical United States. Washington, DC: National Geographic, 2000. Map.

CD-ROM / DVD

Discover the Great Lakes: The Ecosystem of the Great Lakes-St. Lawrence. Ottawa: Environment Canada, 1997. CD-ROM.

The final list of sources for the Huron essay is reproduced below in **Chicago/Turabian style.**

Bibliography

Archaeological Survey of Canada. *The Draper Site*. 20 July 2001. <http://www.civilization.ca/cmc/archeo/oracles/draper/drape.htm> [25 July 2002].

Bonvillain, Nancy. *The Huron*. New York: Chelsea House, 1989.

Castellano, Marlene Brant. "Women in Huron and Ojibwa Societies." *Canadian Woman Studies* 10, no. 2 (1989): 45-48.

Dickason, Olive. *Canada's First Nations: A History of Founding Peoples from Earliest Times*. 3rd ed. Toronto: Oxford University Press, 2002.

Jenness, Diamond. *The Indians of Canada*. 7th ed. Toronto: University of Toronto Press, 1977.

Owen, Roger et al., eds. *The North American Indians*. New York: Macmillan, 1967.

Trigger, Bruce. *The Children of Aataentsic: A History of the Huron People to 1660*. Montreal: McGill-Queen's University Press, 1987.

_____. *Natives and Newcomers: Canada's "Heroic Age" Reconsidered*. Montreal: McGill-Queen's University Press, 1985.

The entry for each source starts at the left margin, with the author's last name mentioned first. If the entry extends beyond the line, the second and subsequent lines are single-spaced and indented five spaces or a paragraph indent. Leave a double space between individual entries. If there is no author, use the title to determine alphabetical order; do not use "anonymous."

When listing two or more sources by the same author, enter the author's name for the first source only. For the next source (and successive sources by the same author) type an eight-space line in place of the author's name followed by a period. The titles of the sources may be arranged alphabetically or chronologically. See the Trigger example above as an illustration.

If you are using a word processor, titles should be italicized. In handwritten or typed essays, titles are underlined.

Art

da Vinci, Leonardo. *The Mona Lisa*. 1506. <http://www.louvre.fr/anglais/collec/peint/inv0779/peint_f.htm> [1 December 2002].

Book

Dickens, Charles. *Great Expectations*. 1861. <http://www.bibliomania.com/0/0/19/frameset.html> [29 November 2002].

Email

Sandler, Judy. <judy@example.com> "Re: Zebra mussels" [Email to Susan Conway <sconway@example.com>]. 6 July 2002.

Encyclopedia

Farr, D.M.L. "The Alaska Boundary Dispute." *The Canadian Encyclopedia*. 2002. <http://www. thecanadianencyclopedia.com/index.cfm> Search: "Alaska Boundary Dispute." [25 October 2002].

General Website

Archaeological Survey of Canada. *The Draper Site*. 20 July 2001. <http://www.civilization. ca/cmc/archeo/ oracles/draper/drape.htm> [10 September 2002].

Journal

Menichetti, David. "German Policy in Occupied Belgium, 1914-1918." *Essays in History* 39. 1997. <http://etext.lib.virginia.edu/journals/EH/EH39/menich39.html> [9 February 2002].

Magazine

Tal, Guy. "Learning to Photograph the Landscape." *Nature Photographers Online Magazine*. September 2002. <http://www.naturephotographers.net/articles0902/gt0902-1.html> [27 November 2002].

Map

The Axis Powers, 1942. N.d. Map. <http://www.indstate.edu/gga/gga_cart/78927.jpg> [13 September 2002].

Newspaper

Schmadeke, Steve. "Fierce flies are deployed to fight Florida fire ants." *Naples Daily News,* 27 November 2002. <http://www.naplesnews.com/02/11/naples/d865261a.htm> [1 December 2002].

Photograph

Simon Wiesenthal Center. *Neville Chamberlain with Adolf Hitler*. 1997. Photograph. <http://motlc.wiesenthal. com/gallery/pg18/pg7/pg18722.html> [22 June 2002].

Professional Website

Crouse, Maurice. *Citing Electronic Information in History Papers*. 18 October 2002. <http://www.people. memphis.edu/~mcrouse/elcite.html> [18 December 2002].

Question and Answer Database

The Chicago Manual of Style. *FAQ (and not so FAQ)*. 2002. <http://www.press.uchicago.edu/Misc/Chicago/ cmosfaq/> [6 December 2002].

Radio / Television

O'Neill, Mark. "Chinese Traditional Medicines." *Quirks and Quarks*. 23 May 1998. <http://www.radio.cbc.ca/ programs/quirks/realaud/may2398.ra> [5 January 2001].

Subscription Database

Woodcock, George. "The Secrets of Her Success." *Quill & Quire* 60. August 1994. *Literature Resource Center*. <http://galenet.galegroup.com/servlet/LitRC> Ottawa Public Library. [2 August 2002].

Explanatory Notes

You acknowledged or cited the sources of your information by using superscript numbers at appropriate places in the text of your essay. The superscript numbers were then linked to either footnotes or endnotes containing details of the cited sources.

There is another type of note that has quite a different function to the citation footnote or endnote. The explanatory note is used for additional information that, while relevant to the essay, might detract from the development of your argument if inserted directly into the text of the essay. For example, you might wish to provide some additional biographical information on a person or define an important term.

The easiest method is to place explanatory information in a footnote at the bottom of the specific page. Simply assign an asterisk (*) or another symbol(†) to the material in the text and place a corresponding symbol at the bottom of the page and provide the explanatory information. An example of an explanatory footnote is shown on page 48 of this guide. The explanatory footnote designated by a symbol works well with both the APA parenthetical procedure and with the numbered endnote system.

However, if you are using footnotes to cite your sources, do not combine numbers (for citing sources) and symbols (for explanatory information). Both numbers and symbols in a set of footnotes will confuse your readers. It is simpler and clearer to use one set of superscript numbers for both citation notes and explanatory notes.

Use explanatory notes sparingly because constant reference to these notes may distract the reader from the development of your argument. Ask yourself whether the information is essential to the essay before using a note. Finally, always strive for **consistency, simplicity, and clarity** in your use of explanatory notes.

Title Page

Reformulate your research question as the title so that it clearly and concisely indicates the focus of the essay. Questions and thesis statements do not substitute for titles. Use a subtitle only if it helps clarify the title. The teacher sees your title page first so ensure that it is clearly and neatly laid out, as shown earlier on pages 22, 32, and 37. The title of the Huron essay could be phrased as follows:

The Huron Trading System

Table of Contents

A contents page provides the reader with an outline of the structure of your essay. Avoid using the term "Body" in the table of contents. It was used in the research and in the outlines to assist you in understanding the structure of an essay. Page numbers are not usually required in a table of contents for an essay or a report.

> ### Contents
>
> A. Introduction
>
> B.
>
>   I. Location
>
>   II. Agriculture
>
>   III. People and Settlements
>
> C. Conclusion
>
> D. Appendix
>
> E. Bibliography

Illustrations

There are two types of illustrations: tables and figures. Examples of tables and figures are shown in the appendix on pages 111–15. Ask yourself whether each table or figure actually illustrates a point in your essay. Illustrations are usually placed at the appropriate place in the text of the essay. If illustrations are too lengthy and detailed and may distract the reader, they can be placed in the appendix.

Appendix

The appendix is a useful place at the end of the essay for important information that is too lengthy to be placed in the body. For example, you might have a detailed chronology of events related to the fur trade that, if placed in the body of the Huron essay, might disrupt the flow of the essay. In that case, place it in the appendix. Guard against the temptation to pack the appendix with unnecessary material. Ensure that all the material in the appendix is relevant to your thesis and that it is cross-referenced by using an explanatory footnote or a parenthetical reference in the essay. Refer to pages 111–18 of this guide for an example of an appendix.

The Final Copy

Ensure that you have included **all the sections and features** of your essay — from title page to bibliography — in your rough draft. Then revise and edit it carefully. Always stay within five percent of the word length stipulated by the teacher. Check once again with your teacher the format for laying out the essay. Allow time in your schedule to set aside your rough draft for a few days before you start the final copy.

Producing the final copy is simply fine tuning the rough draft. All the work that went into the research, outlining, drafting, revising and editing, invariably pays off in the end. The pay off is a quick and painless preparation of the final copy and a top quality research paper.

Remember that the final copy represents just ten percent of the iceberg above the water. However, that ten percent often counts for 100 percent of the final mark. Take care in assembling and packaging the final copy so that it will create a positive initial impact on the reader. **Proofread** the essay thoroughly from title page to bibliography. Ensure that not only have all errors been eliminated but that the final copy is clearly and attractively laid out. It is a good idea to keep a backup hard copy of your essay in case the original is lost.

Preparing your final copy will be even quicker if you have used a computer for revising and editing. The appearance of your essay can also be improved by computer technology. Software programs can ensure a clean, professional type and provide a variety of illustrations. Most schools have computer facilities that are accessible to students, so there is no need to purchase expensive equipment. Although not all teachers require that assignments be done on a computer, combining literary ability with typing and computing skills is an important asset today. Remember, however, that it is **substance,** not technological dazzle, that characterizes a good essay.

5 The Comparative Essay

Comparisons are assigned in many subjects. For example, in English you may be asked to compare two characters in a novel. In geography, you may have to compare the impact of clear-cutting and fires on forest regeneration. In history, you may be required to compare the culture of the Mayan and Inca societies.

Comparisons are more complex than writing the single-focus report or essay described in this guide. In a comparative assignment, you must explain how two individuals, events, or ideas are connected or related. You are required to draw them together in order to show how they are similar and/or different. Create a powerful current so that your comparison will buzz with electrical energy and provide the reader with an insightful, possibly even an original, illumination.

Comparisons are essays with a thesis or argument; they are not narratives, plot summaries, or biographical reports. Descriptive narrative is not comparative analysis.

"Comparing" is widely accepted as including both similarities and differences. For example, "Compare the foreign policies of Canada and the United States between the two World Wars," allows you to focus on either similarities or differences or on a combination of similarities and differences. "Contrasting," however, means concentrating on differences only. For example, "Contrast the roles of the Canadian prime minister and the American president," requires that you focus on the differences only.

Comparative assignments vary. For example, you may be given complete freedom to choose the topic and the focus for comparative analysis or the

assignment may be so specific that even the similarities and/or differences for comparison are prescribed by the teacher. Initially your comparative assignments will be under 1000 words. Major comparative projects involving extensive research are usually only set in senior high school and university.

Therefore, it is especially important to discuss the following questions with your teacher before you start preparing a comparative project:

- Clarify terms like "compare" and "contrast."

- When is the essay due?

- How many sources should be used?

- Should the sources be cited?

- Should the sources be listed?

- How long should the essay be?

- How should the essay be structured?

- How will the assignment be marked?

Let us assume that you are studying the broad topic of "Government and Politics in North America" in your civics class. Your teacher has set a short essay on Canadian and American systems of government and the purpose of the assignment is to: "Compare the Canadian and American systems of government." The teacher has established the following requirements for the comparative essay:

- Encyclopedia articles should be used for the preparatory reading.

- Four sources should be used (two Canadian and two American).

- No citations are needed.

- A list of the sources (bibliography) is required.

- The length should be between 700 and 800 words.

- One month has been set aside for the project.

The pathway opposite shows the stages for preparing your comparative essay on the Canadian and American systems of government. This pathway can be followed for comparative assignments in a wide variety of subjects, whether you are required to focus on similarities and/or differences. You will notice that the process is similar to the method described for preparing the report and the different types of essays. Although a Working Outline is not normally part of the preparation process for essays, comparative essays do require a preliminary outline of similarities and/or differences.

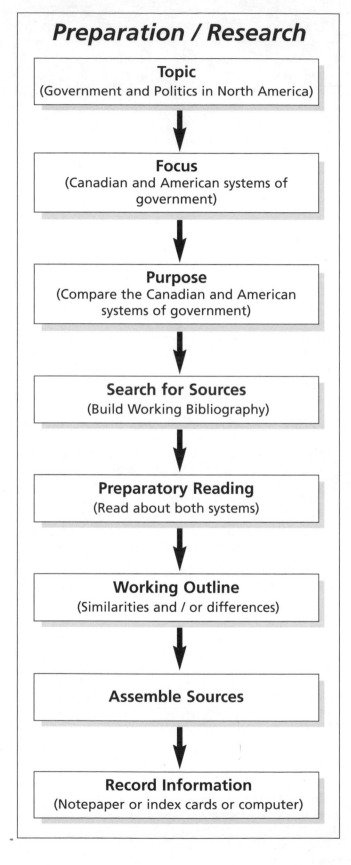

Preparation / Research

Topic
(Government and Politics in North America)

↓

Focus
(Canadian and American systems of government)

↓

Purpose
(Compare the Canadian and American systems of government)

↓

Search for Sources
(Build Working Bibliography)

↓

Preparatory Reading
(Read about both systems)

↓

Working Outline
(Similarities and / or differences)

↓

Assemble Sources

↓

Record Information
(Notepaper or index cards or computer)

PREPARATION

In our comparative example, the teacher has prescribed the specific requirements for the assignment. If you are permitted to select your own topic and narrow the focus, simply follow the familiar pathway on the previous page. Establishing the purpose is straightforward because a comparative assignment implies a basic question: What are the similarities and/or differences and how are they linked? Compiling a short Working Bibliography will be quick and easy for students with advanced research skills.

Preparatory reading is essential for a comparative essay. Because there is a double focus in a comparative essay, you must have a thorough understanding of **both** aspects or elements **before** you start recording information. Encyclopedia articles are especially useful for the preparatory reading because they offer a broad survey. Read through the encyclopedia articles familiarizing yourself with the two systems of government in our example. As you read, keep the purpose of the assignment in mind.

The purpose in our example is to "Compare the Canadian and American systems of government." Therefore, you would be trying to identify both similarities and differences in the two systems of government. These similarities and differences would be noted on separate pages in your *I.Q. Journal* as shown in the adjacent column. This tentative list of similarities and differences represents a loose Working Outline that is necessary **before** you start to record the relevant information and ideas to develop the comparison.

Do not bypass the preparatory reading because the invisible foundations of the iceberg are even more important for a comparative essay than for the single-focus essay. Once you have a good grasp of what is to be compared and a tentative list of similarities and/or differences, you are ready to move on to the next stage.

Assemble the sources listed in your Working Bibliography. Then prepare your notetaking system. Like the report and the earlier essays, an **organized system for recording your ideas and information is crucial** for a successful comparative assignment. Because you are linking two separate elements or features, the notetaking system is not exactly the same as the system used in the single-focus report and essays. You can use either notepaper, index cards, or a computer. These methods are described in detail on the following pages. Unless the teacher stipulates the method, consider trying one of the following three methods that you have not used before in order to broaden your research experience.

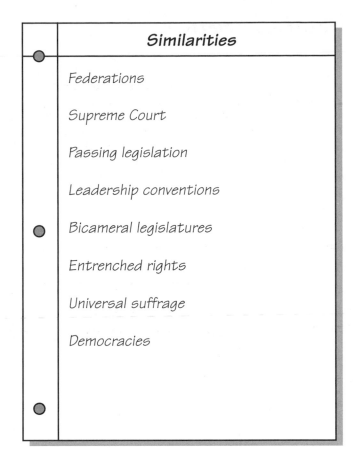

Similarities

Federations

Supreme Court

Passing legislation

Leadership conventions

Bicameral legislatures

Entrenched rights

Universal suffrage

Democracies

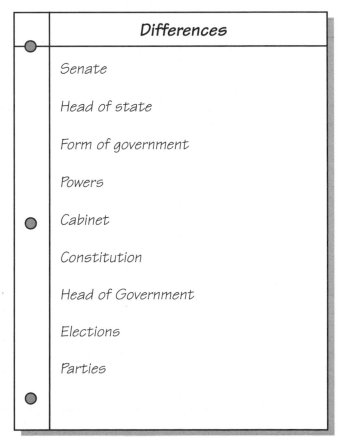

Differences

Senate

Head of state

Form of government

Powers

Cabinet

Constitution

Head of Government

Elections

Parties

Notepaper Method

Set up notepaper pages headed "Similarities" and "Differences," as shown below and on the following page. Notice that the **columns are structured differently** on each page. You have already isolated a tentative list of similarities and differences in your *I.Q. Journal* as a starting point. You need these similarities and differences as magnets to help select the relevant information needed to make comparisons. Simply writing down reams of notes, on the off-chance that some links and connections may emerge, just wastes time.

Read carefully through your first source, looking specifically for information that represents either a similarity or a difference in the practices of Canadian and American styles of government. Record the information on either the "Similarities" or the "Differences" page. List the main categories, for example "Supreme Court" and "Senate," in the similarities or differences columns. List the explanatory details and examples in the adjoining columns.

There must be matching categories with corresponding examples and details from both Canada and the United States to make a comparison possible. **You cannot compare something with nothing.** Do not write down any notes unless the information is linked to a major similarity or difference that applies to **both** Canadian and American systems of government.

Similarities	Canada / U.S.
Supreme Court	interprets the constitution
Federation	provinces and states
Entrenched rights	Charter of Rights and Bill of Rights
Senate	Same name; protects provinces and states
Money bills	introduced in Commons and House of Reps
Democracies	universal suffrage
Bicameral	Commons and Senate; House of Reps and Senate
Committees	important in the legislative process
Legislation	3 readings in each house
Cabinet	supervises gov. departments
Supreme Court	9 judges including a Chief Justice
Constitution	partly written in Canada; entirely written in U.S.

Read through your next source looking for similarities and differences and record the details as just explained. Your sources (unless they are comparative studies) will not provide you with the similarities and differences. You will have to establish the connections as you work through your sources. Read all your sources carefully, applying your creative imagination as you search for links. Then record the information on your notepaper as shown.

You should continue to discover more major similarities and differences while you are reading and recording. Add these similarities and differences to the list in your *I.Q. Journal* and use them as a basis to help reveal more links and details as you research.

Since our example is not a major research paper and you are not required to cite your sources, there is no need to indicate the source of each note with a code and page number. **Write on one side of the notepaper and leave a line between each note.** This will enable you to separate the individual notes with scissors later when you are ready to start structuring your answer.

Canada	Differences	U.S.
appointed by p.m.; 104 members	Senate	elected; 2x50=100
constitutional monarchy	Form of gov.	republic
monarch, gov-general	Head of State	president
elected and responsible to Commons	Cabinet	not in Congress; aptd. by pres
prime minister, elected member of Commons	Head of Gov.	pres., may not sit in Congress
within 5 years	Elections	fixed terms
weak	Senate	powerful
vote of no-confidence	Removal of Head of Gov.	impeach
unlimited number of terms	Head of Gov.	two terms only
not influential	Senate (legislation)	important

Index Card Method

If you use index cards for recording your information instead of notepaper, **each** similarity and/or difference must be written on a **separate card.** Assign a heading — one of the major similarities and/or differences from the list in your *I.Q. Journal* — in the top right-hand corner of the card. See the "Senate" card opposite as an example. Indicate in brackets after the heading whether it is a similarity (S) or a difference (D). Then write the explanatory details and examples in the space below.

In the case of differences, there might be more details so you would have to continue some notes on the reverse side of the cards. Try to avoid using two index cards for one similarity or difference. You can use abbreviations for the headings to save time: for example, "HofG." for "Head of Government."

Alternatively, you can use coloured index cards. For example, use green cards for similarities and blue cards for differences. There is no need to use the designations (S) and (D) if you classify your cards by colour. But you must still assign a heading, for example "HofG" or "Senate" to each card.

You will notice that there are differences between the index card method described earlier for the research essay and the method described here for the comparative essay. Since our example is not a major comparative research paper and citations are not required, there is no need to indicate the source code and page reference for each note.

Although the list of similarities and differences in our *I.Q. Journal* represents a loose Working Outline, **do not assign numbers** to these similarities and differences at this stage, as recommended for the major sections on page 50. Insert a heading, not a number, on each card, as shown opposite. The section numbers will be assigned when a firmer structure emerges at the Basic Outline stage.

Computer Method

You can also use a computer for recording the information for a comparative essay. Modify your "notepaper" files to reflect the structure shown on pages 74–75 or use electronic "index cards." Then follow the instructions above for recording your electronic notes. If you are feeling confident about your research skills, why not experiment and design your own process for creating your electronic notes? Remember our earlier advice that, if you can modify the suggestions in the manual, then by all means do so and **shape your own research pathways.**

Senate (S)

Same name; protects provinces and states

HofG. (D)

Canada: prime minister; elected member of Commons

U.S.: president; may not sit in Congress

Sometimes it is quicker and more effective to use diagrams rather than text in your notes to demonstrate a similarity or a difference. See the example below. It shows overlapping powers in Canada and the separation of powers in the United States.

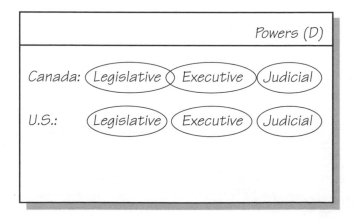

Powers (D)

Canada: (Legislative) (Executive) (Judicial)

U.S.: (Legislative) (Executive) (Judicial)

PRESENTATION

If you are using notepaper, take a pair of scissors and separate the individual notes. **Keep the "Similarities" and "Differences" apart.** Take the separated "Similarities" notes and spread them out on a table. Then group the notepaper strips into major categories. For example, all notes about similarities between the Canadian and American Supreme Courts should be grouped together, as shown below.

Supreme Court	interprets the constitution
Supreme Court	9 judges including a Chief Justice
Supreme Court	powerful role because of entrenched rights

Once you have organized your "Similarities," go through the strips of paper denoting "Differences" and group them into common categories, as shown below. Use paper clips to keep them together.

appointed by pm; 104 members	Senate	elected; 2x50=100 members
weak	Senate	powerful
not influential	Senate (legislation	important

Follow exactly the same method if you are using index cards. Each card will have a heading followed by an (S) or a (D) or they may be colour coded, making them easy to separate. Group them in common categories like the strips of notepaper. Use rubber bands to keep the cards together.

Never mix similarities and differences in one group. In other words, notes dealing with differences between the Senates should be kept separate from those dealing with similarities in the two Senates.

If you are using a computer to record your information, you could print your notes, cut them and then sort them manually as explained. Alternatively, you could sort and group them electronically by cutting and pasting.

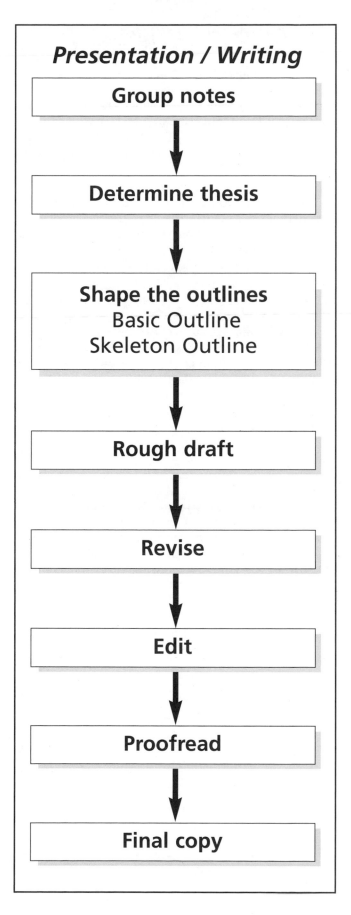

Presentation / Writing

Group notes

⬇

Determine thesis

⬇

Shape the outlines
Basic Outline
Skeleton Outline

⬇

Rough draft

⬇

Revise

⬇

Edit

⬇

Proofread

⬇

Final copy

Once you have grouped your notes and identified the major similarities and differences, you have to decide whether the similarities or the differences dominate the relationship. There may be an equal mix of similarities and differences. These are important considerations because they will **determine your thesis and the structure of your answer.**

After grouping your notes, you may find that one section has far more information than all the others. For example, you may have so much information (both similarities and differences) on the Senate that you may wish to focus your essay just on the Canadian and American Senates. However, do not narrow the focus of your comparison unless your teacher has approved the change.

In our example, there are considerably more major differences than similarities. It is logical then to focus the essay on the differences between the Canadian and American systems of government. Because this is a short assignment, you may not be able to cover all the differences. The next step is to **select the most important differences** to illustrate the thesis that the Canadian and American systems of government are different and distinct.

These differences will form the body of the Basic Outline, as shown below. Designate each section with a "D" to signify a difference. Once the Basic Outline is established, the next step is to structure the Skeleton Outline. In exactly the same way as described earlier in the manual, read through the notes of each section of the Basic Outline separately. Then choose the relevant information needed to develop the comparison for each section. Remember that there must be matching categories and corresponding examples from the practice of government in **both** Canada and the United States to draw comparisons.

Basic Outline

A. Introduction
B.   I. Elections (D)
    II. Head of Government (D)
    III. Head of State (D)
    IV. Cabinet
    V. Legislation
    VI. Senate (D)
C. Conclusion

Skeleton Outline

A. Introduction
  1. Background
  2. Thesis

B.
  I. Elections (D)
    1. Regular intervals / within 5 years
    2. Senate, House of Reps, Pres. / only Commons

  II. Head of Government (D)
    1. Pres. elected / PM elected leader of majority party
    2. Pres. not in Congress / PM in Commons
    3. Removal: impeachment / no-confidence

  III. Head of State (D)
    1. Republic / Monarchy
    2. Combined in Pres. / separate in Can.

  IV. Cabinet (D)
    1. Not in Congress / members of Commons
    2. Influence differs re legislation

  V. Legislation (D)
    1. Often deadlocked / smoother passage
    2. Ex. not at fault / PM + Cab. responsible

  VI. Senate (D)
    1. U.S. elected / Can. apptd.
    2. Powerful / weak

C. Conclusion

As in the earlier report and the essays, the outlines provide a formula for developing the paragraphs. In a short assignment of less than 1000 words — whether it is a report, an essay or a comparison — the Basic Outline will establish the paragraph structure, as shown below.

The Skeleton Outline, shown in the previous column, will provide the supporting details for each

Basic Outline

A. Introduction   (Paragraph)

B.   I. Elections (D)   (Paragraph)

      II. Head of   (Paragraph)
         Government (D)

      III. Head of State (D) (Paragraph)

      IV. Cabinet   (Paragraph)

      V. Legislation   (Paragraph)

      VI. Senate (D)   (Paragraph)

C. Conclusion   (Paragraph)

A comparative study is not a report — it is an essay with a thesis or argument. Therefore, you cannot just describe whatever you are comparing, such as the Canadian and American systems of government. You have to **explain the links and the relationships** clearly. You cannot expect your readers to figure out the connections. Remember the analogy of the electrical current flowing between each major category. The absence of electricity will create a blackout, leaving the reader groping in the dark trying to figure out the connections.

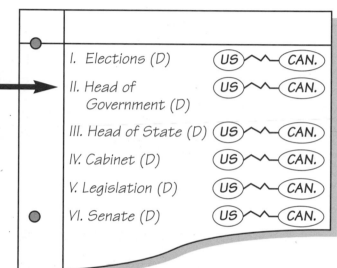

paragraph. Once you have your structure mapped out with the supporting details, it is easy to write the rough draft. Remember:

- Write clearly and correctly.

- Introduce the essay effectively.

- Organize the paragraphs around a central focal point.

- Demonstrate the similarities and/or differences with corresponding examples.

- Ensure that all information and observations are relevant to your thesis.

- Sum up your conclusions in the final paragraph.

- Set up the title page.

- Format the list of sources.

- Revise and edit the rough draft.

- Proofread the final copy.

A Comparative Study of Government in Canada and the United States

Judy Sandler
Social Studies 2A

Ms Helen Thexton
15 May 2002

The Americans successfully fought a revolutionary war against the British to gain their independence. In 1787 the delegates representing the victorious states designed a distinctly American constitution. Canada, on the other hand, followed a peaceful and evolutionary route. In the slow process of advancing to independence, Canada adopted many features of British Parliamentary government. But Canada also shares a continent with the United States and it has been influenced by its dominant neighbour in numerous ways. Although Canada and the United States of America may have many common characteristics, history has shaped two different and distinctive systems of government.

Elections are one major difference. The Americans hold biennial federal elections in November. The House of Representatives and one-third of the Senate are elected every two years. The president is elected every four years. In Canada elections are not held at fixed intervals. The Constitution requires that an election must be called within five years of the previous election. In a federal election members are elected to the House of Commons only. American elections are called at fixed times for specified terms, unlike the more flexible Canadian system.

The roles of the prime minister and the president as heads of government are also different. In Canada, the prime minister is the leader of the party that controls a majority of seats in the House of Commons. By tradition the prime minister must be an elected member of the Commons. The president is elected directly by the people and by a special mechanism called the Electoral College, but is not permitted to sit in either house of the Congress. The only way to remove an American president is by impeachment, but a Canadian prime minister can be forced to resign by a vote of no-confidence in the House of Commons.

Another difference between the two forms of government is that Canada is a constitutional monarchy, while the United States is a republic. The Americans have combined the positions of head of state and head of government in the presidency. In Canada the positions are separate: the monarch, represented by the governor-general, is head of state and the prime minister is head of government. However, it is the prime minister who actually chooses the governor-general. The president and prime minister may have different roles but they are both powerful figures.

Although the cabinets are appointed by the president and prime minister and cabinet members administer the government departments, the cabinets function differently in each country. Like the president, the American cabinet is not permitted to sit in the Congress. This allows the president to select experts from all over the country. In Canada, the prime minister is required by tradition to select the cabinet from the elected members of the House of Commons. Therefore, the Canadian cabinet has an influential role in shaping and passing the laws. The appointed American cabinet does not have the same power in shaping legislation as the elected Canadian cabinet.

Although the process of passing bills into law is similar, there are other legislative differences. Since the prime minister and cabinet launch the bills in a house that they control, they can usually guide these bills through fairly easily. The Canadian Senate may stall a bill but will seldom reject it outright. The governor-general automatically signs into law all bills passed by both houses. Passage of legislation in the United States is seldom as smooth a process. Legislation is often deadlocked for months because control of the Congress and the presidency may be in the hands of different political parties. A law in its final form may be quite different from the original bill. The prime minister and cabinet have more power than their American counterparts in passing legislation. There is a price though: if a major bill fails to pass in the Commons, the prime minister and cabinet have to resign and another election is called. Failure of a bill in the Congress cannot be blamed on the president and cabinet.

Other than the name, the two Senates have little in common. The one hundred members of the American Senate (two representatives from each of the fifty states) are elected for a term of six years each. One third of the Senate is elected every two years so that the composition of the membership is rotated. The Canadian senators (104) are appointed by the prime minister to serve until they reach seventy-five years of age. American senators can block and strike down bills while the Canadian Senate can only delay legislation. Furthermore, the American Constitution has

given the Senate important powers, such as approving all foreign treaties. The elected American Senate, representing all the states equally, is a more powerful body than the appointed Canadian Senate.

Increasingly Canada is influenced by American cultural values, but the past still has an enduring influence on the political system. Although there are some similarities between our systems of government, differences, such as those described, still dominate in the most important aspects of government in the United States and Canada.

Bibliography

Beaudoin, G.A. "Constitutional Law." *Canadian Encylopedia.* 2nd ed.

Guy, James, J. *How We are Governed: the Basics of Canadian Politics and Government.* Toronto: Harcourt Brace, 1995.

Harris, James T. "United States of America: The Structure of Government." *Encyclopedia Britannica: Macropaedia.* 15th ed.

Welch, Susan et al. *Understanding American Government.* 4th ed. Belmont, CA: Wadsworth, 1997.

The sample essay above is based on the structure of the Basic Outline on page 78 and the paragraphs reflect this structure. The supporting details for each paragraph are derived from the Skeleton Outline which is also shown on page 78. You will notice that the essay has an **introduction** with a clear thesis statement: differences dominate the two systems of government. The differences are linked and developed in the **body** and there is a short **conclusion.** A title page and a bibliography have also been provided. There is no need for a table of contents in a short assignment.

EXAMINATIONS

Comparative essay questions are common in examinations and they are also frequently set as in-class assignments in a variety of subjects. Sometimes the questions are set in advance and you are permitted to bring an outline into the examination room or you may be given no advance knowledge of the questions.

If you have prepared and written comparative essays during your courses, you will not find comparative examination questions or in-class assignments intimidating. The techniques of comparative analysis demonstrated in the preparation and presentation of the Canadian-American government example are much the same in an examination setting.

Let us assume that you are writing a final examination in your English course. Your teacher has informed you that there will be a comparative section on Arthur Miller's play, *Death of a Salesman*, which you have studied in class. There will be four questions in the section and you have to select one.

Once the examination paper is handed out, read the questions carefully before making your selection. Suppose you choose the following question:

"Compare the characterizations of Biff and Happy in Arthur Miller's play, *Death of a Salesman.*"

- "Compare" allows you to focus on either similarities or differences or a combination of both similarities and differences.

- When selecting your question, it is essential that you have a thorough understanding of **both** characters.

- Calculate the amount of time you can spend on the question according to how many marks it is worth.

- Allow five to ten minutes to plan the structure of your answer. Do not start writing until you have mapped out the structure.

- Brainstorm the major similarities and differences between the two characters. Jot the similarities and differences down in two separate columns.

- Decide whether similarities or differences dominate.

- Determining the extent of the similarities and differences will shape both your thesis and the structure of the answer.

- Select the most important similarities and/or differences and create the Basic Outline.

- Link and demonstrate the similarities and/or differences with specific examples from both characters.

- Set up the Skeleton Outline with the supporting details.

- You do not have enough time to write a rough draft in an examination.

- Keep the introduction short and ensure that the thesis is clearly and concisely stated.

- Develop and substantiate the thesis in the body by explicitly linking the similarities and/or differences between the characters.

- Draw the comparative threads together in a concluding paragraph.

- Base the paragraph structure on the Basic Outline.

- Avoid subheadings.

- Write in a clear, correct style.

- Remember that the clarity of your answer is shaped largely by its structure and style.

- Write legibly.

- Allow time at the end to proofread your answer.

Tips

Style is the manner of your writing, rather than the content of your essay.[11] It is the written expression of your ideas, not the ideas themselves. Although it is difficult to separate language from ideas — "Expression and content are white and yolk in a scrambled egg"[12] — you must concentrate on developing a clear, pleasing style. These "tips" on writing style will help you achieve clarity of expression, the key feature of good style.

- **Use simple and direct language.** Avoid fancy words when plain words will serve your purpose. State your point simply and clearly. If you are describing a mollusk that has dark and light stripes, do not say it has "alternating tenebrous and canescent bands." Say "it is striped like a zebra."

- **Eliminate vague and meaningless words.** If it is unclear what you are trying to say, replace the word or words with more definite ones. For example, "The zebra mussel is a small striped creature," is not as precise as "The zebra mussel is a brown and white mollusk about 2.5 cm in length." By replacing the vague words "small," "striped," and "creature" with more concrete words, the reader has a clearer picture of the zebra mussel. Etcetera (etc.) is a meaningless term and should never be used in a report or an essay.

- **Omit needless words and phrases.** Every word in a sentence should serve a purpose. If a word seems unnecessary, try to eliminate or replace it. For example, "In spite of the fact that . . . " can be stated more simply as "Although . . ."

- **Check the fluency of your writing.** Good writing has an even, easy flow like harmonious music. Test your writing by reading it aloud. If you have difficulty reading your projects, edit the text. Linking words, such as "therefore" and "consequently" can improve the rhythm of your writing and combine and balance your sentences.

- **Keep your tone formal.** The tone of your assignment is the expression of your own voice in your writing. Because reports and essays are serious pieces of writing, your tone should be formal but sincere. Therefore, you should not use casual or slang language that you might use with your friends. For example, you would not write this: "Zebra mussels are a big problem. But what the heck, all that garbage we dump into the Great Lakes is a humungus problem too." The point would be better expressed this way: "Zebra mussels are a major problem, but when you consider all the garbage we mindlessly — and often lawlessly — dump into the Great Lakes, they are certainly not the only problem."

- **Use active verbs instead of passive verbs.** Active verbs are more forceful and concise than passive verbs. It is better to state "Zebra mussels *invaded* the Great Lakes" than "The Great Lakes *were invaded* by zebra mussels."

- **Make sure those active verbs are consistent in tense.** Reports and essays are usually written in the past tense, except for literary essays which use the present tense. Do not shift from "is" to "was" and from "are" to "were" throughout the essay.

- **Avoid using contractions.** Using words such as "do not" instead of "don't" or "cannot" in place of "can't" keeps your writing formal. You will notice that this guide does not use contractions.

- **Check for correct spelling.** Keep a dictionary at your side to help you when you are unsure of the spelling of a word. If you are using a computer, make use of the spell check but do not rely on it entirely because some computer software may not be able to tell whether you should use "too," "two," or "to."

- **Choose your words carefully.** The development and clear expression of an idea depends largely on your selection and use of words. A dictionary and a thesaurus will help you expand your vocabulary. They will also help you achieve precision as well as avoid repetition. Instead of repeatedly using the verb "trade," you could replace it with words like "barter" or "exchange." Expand your vocabulary by compiling glossaries and lists of new words.

- **Vary the length of your sentences.** Mixing longer sentences with shorter ones changes the pace of your writing. This will liven up your writing. Shorter sentences can be used to give emphasis and it is also effective to place the key words at the end of a sentence.

- **Choose your pronouns carefully.** Although instructional guides, such as this one often use the pronouns "you" and "we," you should avoid using "you" or "we" and use "I" sparingly in your projects. Some teachers object to the use of "I," so always consult your teacher. Instead of "I" some teachers prefer "the author" or "the writer."

- **Use abbreviations carefully.** You may use abbreviations, such as UN for the United Nations, as long as you identify them in parentheses when you first use them.

- **Pay attention to your punctuation.** Proper punctuation will make your sentences flow and help clarify your meaning. Common errors are misuse of commas and run-on sentences.

- **Learn correct grammar.** Using the rules of language appropriately will improve the clarity of your writing. Make use of the grammar check on your computer.

- **Avoid sexist language.** Do not use language that excludes women. Saying "An American senator is usually the best man for the job because he is elected by the people" excludes all female senators. It is better to rephrase the sentence as follows: "Because American senators are elected by the people, they are usually the most suitable for the job." Sometimes it is just a matter of substituting a word like police officer for policeman.

- **Add reference books** to your collection, such as a dictionary, a thesaurus, a grammar manual, a guide to non-sexist language, and a handbook of style.

Revising and Editing

Once you have completed your draft you are ready to start revising and editing. Revising involves reviewing the **structure,** while editing is fine tuning the **style** of the revised draft. These are important stages and you must allow time for them in your schedule. It is also a good time to gather your group again to help revise and edit one another's drafts.

Your first task is to examine the order of the main sections of the body as you revise the rough draft. The question to ask yourself is whether there is a smooth, logical flow in the sequence of the sections. Check the introduction to make sure that both the purpose and your point of view are clearly spelled out. Does the conclusion serve its purpose?

Once you are satisfied with the structure, look closely at the paragraphing. Circle the topic sentence in each paragraph to ensure that there is a central focal point. Is there sufficient supporting detail in each paragraph? Is there unity to each paragraph? Have you eliminated unnecessary words and phrases? Do the quotations blend in? Are the paragraphs linked by transitional words or phrases? These are the questions you should ask yourself as you revise your draft. But above all, make certain that the essay develops **a clear point of view.**

Editing is the fine tuning and polishing of your draft. Use the style "Tips" as a checklist when you edit. Crisp, clear expression will lend an authority to your ideas. When you have completed the editing, ask a member of your group to read the draft and suggest improvements.

The next step is to read your draft aloud. You can read it to yourself or tape record it. You may read it to your group or to a friend. Perhaps someone else could read it while you listen. If your essay sounds rough, you will have to edit it and remove the "static" until it flows smoothly and naturally.[13] Give your teachers the sensation of gliding along in a rowing shell — not bouncing in an old truck on a rough road — as they read your projects.

A computer is a valuable writing tool. It can speed up the revising and editing process, and enhance the quality of your writing assignments. The advantage of a computer is that once the information is typed, revision and editing can be done without retyping the draft.

It is not always easy to get a feel for the overall structure of an essay on a computer monitor, nor is it easy to detect punctuation or spelling errors. You should revise and edit on a printed copy of the draft as well as on the electronic version. Another advantage of a printed copy is being able to read it aloud. Members of

your group can also read and check it. You can then make the changes on the computer and print another copy for further editing.

If you are revising and editing on a computer, you may wish to keep all your electronic drafts. In this case simply name each revision, such as "Huron1," "Huron2," and so on. This will allow you to return to earlier versions for material that you deleted in later revisions. After you have produced your final copy, you can delete the earlier files. Alternatively, you could keep printed copies of earlier versions.

Whether you are printing copies or revising and editing on the computer, it is important that you frequently save your draft on both the hard drive and on a disk to avoid losing the essay if there is a power failure or your hard drive malfunctions. Teachers no longer accept the excuse that the computer "crashed."

If your software program has a spell check, thesaurus and/or a grammar check feature, take advantage of them when you are editing. Remember that you must edit your work carefully even after you have used a computer. Misused words, unclear language and gaps in reasoning can elude the most powerful software.

Vocabulary

Clear thinking and successful learning are only possible with a good command of language. And language mastery is largely determined by our command of vocabulary. Words are the building blocks of language.[14] Below are listed a number of strategies for enriching your vocabulary.

1. Prefixes

Prefix:	Meaning:	Example:	Definition:
inter	between	international	between nations

2. Root words

Root:	Meaning:	Example:	Definition:
bios	life	biology	study of life

3. Homophones

Build a list of similar sounding words that have different meanings, such as:

- aisle/isle
- principle/principal
- complement/compliment

Add meanings and sample sentences.

4. Similar looking words

Many similar looking words cause confusion, such as:

- flaunt/flout
- enormous/enormity
- partake/participate

Add meanings and sample sentences.

5. Synonyms and antonyms

Build lists showing words with both similar and opposite meanings.

6. Glossaries

Assign a section in your notebook or binder for each subject and build a list of terms and definitions specific to that subject. For example, in English you could list and define literary devices, such as mood, plot, and setting. In history, you could list political terms, such as republic, monarchy, and bicameral.

7. Vocabulary journal

Devote a separate binder or notebook to developing a general vocabulary list. Assign a letter of the alphabet to each page and jot down interesting and challenging words on the appropriate page as you encounter them in your studies. Write down the meaning and illustrate the word in a sample sentence to reinforce your understanding of each one.

8. Foreign phrases

Words and phrases from other languages are frequently used in English. Examples include:

- status quo
- coup d'etat
- junta

Build a list with meanings and sample sentences.

Writers are not born; they develop their craft through reading widely and practising their writing constantly. Developing your writing skills is no different from perfecting any skills — it requires effort and practice. It is worth the effort because a **good command of language is invaluable, both for school and for life.**

Public Speaking

Teachers use a variety of public speaking activities in the classroom. These include reciting poems, story telling, seminars, tutorials, small group discussions, interviews, debating, speeches, panel discussions, simulations, and role playing. Some of these are individual activities, while others are conducted in pairs or groups. Some presentations may be complemented by audio-visual aids, others involve memorization, while some entail improvisation. Question and answer sessions sometimes follow certain presentations.

1. SPEECHES

Speeches range from prepared informative speeches to persuasive speeches to impromptu speeches. An informative speech will be used to illustrate how a speech can be prepared. You can apply the same process to prepare most types of speeches. The informative speech is the oral equivalent of a written report. Like a report, an informative speech is explanatory and descriptive; it does not present an argument or point of view. Just as in written presentations, it is essential to do the preparatory work for oral presentations, such as speeches. The analogy of the iceberg applies equally to both written and oral presentations.

By revisiting the zebra mussel project, the similarities between preparing a written report and an informative speech can be clearly illustrated. Suppose your teacher has asked you to prepare a five minute informative speech on an aspect of the zebra mussel problem in the Great Lakes. You would go through the same process of narrowing the focus, formulating your question or purpose and doing the research. If you practise the research skills in both your written assignments as well as your public speaking presentations, you will be zipping along your research pathway by the time you graduate.

The process for preparing a written report and an informative speech is similar right up to the detailed outlines. For a five minute speech, a Skeleton Outline will provide you with an adequate structure. A longer speech will require a Point-form Outline similar to the one on page 55.

Structure is just as important when delivering a speech as it is when composing an essay. Once you have converted the research for your speech into a concise Skeleton or Point-form Outline, you will have all the essential information structured according to the ABC formula. For oral presentations the amount of detail included will have to be carefully controlled so that your audience is not overwhelmed.

The introduction, making up about ten percent of the speech, consists of important background information, a statement of the focus of the speech (for example, the zebra mussel problem in Lake Erie), and a clear indication of the purpose ("The purpose of my presentation is to describe the impact of the zebra mussels on Lake Erie").

The body, as in a written assignment, forms the bulk of the speech and is devoted entirely to developing the answer to your question or purpose. Like a written report, the answer to your question represents the theme of your speech. Finally, the conclusion sums up the main points and concludes your presentation. Remember not to add any new information in the conclusion.

There is no need to prepare a rough copy because that might encourage you to memorize or read the speech. Memorizing the speech may make you sound mechanical, or, worse, forget a crucial point and panic. Simply reading your speech may put your audience to sleep. An organized ABC outline will allow you to communicate your ideas and information more effectively. Using index cards to deliver your speech may, because of the need to flip through them, distract your audience; worse still, you may become distracted if you drop one of the cards or they get out of order.

A better method is to reduce your outline (Skeleton or Point-form) to key words and write the shortened outline on a page of notepaper or on a piece of firm white cardboard. With the overall structure and supporting details of your speech mapped out in front of you, you will be able to talk to your audience without fear of distraction. Circle the main sections of your outline and highlight the subsections in different colours for quick and easy reference. You can also jot down suggestions for delivery in the margin, such as when to pause and where to repeat important information.

Rehearsing is essential for successful speeches. Try to record your presentation and then listen to it to detect weaknesses. Rehearsing in front of a mirror is another option. You could also arrange for some friends to act as an audience and comment on your presentation. A video will allow you to review your delivery and fine tune your "body language" (gestures, posture, and facial expressions). If possible, attempt at least one rehearsal in the room where the presentation will take place. Consider doing visualization exercises where you picture yourself delivering a successful speech. Careful preparation and rehearsing will not only improve your presentation, it will also build your self-confidence.

A speech is built on two pillars: **content and delivery.** Communicating your message (the **content**) clearly to your audience is your most important task. Just like a written assignment, the structure and the style of your speech will determine its clarity. The structure is provided by the outline, while style represents the manner of your **delivery**, which is largely shaped by your voice and body language. The following suggestions will help you improve the delivery of your speech.

- Use precise, formal language.

- Choose your words carefully.

- Pronounce your words clearly.

- Vary the volume and tone of your voice.

- Vary the pace of your delivery.

- Pause occasionally for emphasis.

- Maintain eye contact with your audience.

- Stand (or sit) erect.

- Avoid nervous mannerisms, such as swaying or rocking.

- Use humour sparingly.

- Be enthusiastic.

- Avoid excessive hand gestures.

- Breathe naturally.

- Dress appropriately.

- Be natural, sincere, and relaxed.

- Conclude with confidence.

Do not distribute any supplementary material, such as handouts, before or during your speech. It will only distract your audience.

Visual aids can give added impact to your presentation. The next section lists a number of multimedia techniques, some of which you may wish to use to supplement your presentation. However, you must always keep the spotlight on yourself: you are the star. Remember that technology is only a tool used to support what you are presentin; it is not the focus of your presentation.

Informative speeches in the classroom are often followed by a discussion. If you are asked a question and do not know the answer, it is safer to acknowledge not knowing the answer than to try to fake an answer. Instead, offer to find the answer later.

Teachers frequently combine written and oral presentations. After an oral presentation, and the subsequent discussion, the teacher may require that a written report or essay be submitted. The comments and feedback from this discussion can help you to prepare the final written submission. Sometimes the teacher will ask the class to compile individual written comments on the presentations which can then be used by the presenter to prepare the written report or essay. Fellow students can provide insight, advice, support, and inspiration — and they are right in the classroom with you.

The teacher will probably assess a classroom speech if it is on a topic that is part of the course. Attached is a sample form that can be used for judging speeches. It is not uncommon for members of the class to also evaluate other students' speeches on a similar form.

You will find that the process and the skills involved in preparing and presenting speeches can be modified and applied to other public speaking presentations, such as simulations, seminars, and debating. Like writing, **public speaking is a valuable life-skill.**

SPEECHES

Speaker: _____ Judge: _____

Topic / Title: _____

Criteria \ Levels	Weak	Satisfactory	Good	Very Good	Excellent	TOTAL /50
Introduction						/5
Knowledge / Understanding						/5
Clarity of content						/5
Structure / Organization						/5
Conclusion / Summation						/5
Expression / Language						/5
Control of voice						/5
Enthusiasm / Sincerity						/5
Confidence / Poise						/5
Audience interest						/5

2. MULTIMEDIA PRESENTATIONS

Listed below are some means by which you can supplement your presentation. Knowing how to use multimedia equipment is another useful skill today. Remember, however, that these tools and techniques should complement, not dominate, your oral presentation.

- Models
- Chalkboard / Whiteboard
- Charts
- Graphs
- Art work
- Artifacts
- Diagrams
- Flip charts
- Posters
- Handouts
- Maps
- Photographs
- Overhead projector
- Video / Film
- Slide projector
- Guest speakers
- Music
- CD / Tape / MP3 player
- VCR / TV
- Simulations
- Role playing
- Costumes
- DVD player
- Presentation software (e.g. Microsoft PowerPoint)
- Video projector
- Multimedia computer

3. SEMINARS

Speeches can range from the prepared informative and persuasive to the impromptu and extemporaneous. The prepared informative speech, as just explained, is similar to the written report — both are explanatory and develop a neutral theme. The persuasive speech is the oral equivalent of the written essay — both develop a thesis, argument, or point of view. In the classroom setting, the persuasive speech, coupled with a discussion, is commonly known as a seminar.

Seminars* are widely used in senior high school and university but are less common in junior high school. However, a modified seminar approach, known as a "viewpoint," is often used in current affairs programs in the early high school years. The process for preparing a viewpoint is similar to preparing an informative speech but the presentation is slightly different because the emphasis is on developing and substantiating a point of view or argument.

- Students each select a current national or international issue.
- Students each formulate a research question.
- Students research and prepare their points of view.
- Students develop Skeleton Outlines.
- Students present their viewpoints for three to five minutes.
- Teacher (or a student) chairs the discussion following the presentation.

Be an **active listener** by concentrating on the speaker's presentation, taking notes, and jotting down questions. During the discussion, pose your questions or make thoughtful comments on the issues raised by the speaker. Always respect the opinions and ideas of others, even though you may disagree with them. Controversial issues and problems will always raise a range of interpretations and frequently you will just have to agree to disagree. Never allow yourself to become an "empty barrel" who sounds off at every opportunity and tries to monopolize the discussion. Active listening and an open mind will lead to thoughtful responses and questions.

A key element of any type of oral presentation is the rapport or the bond that you establish with your audience. Mastering the techniques and strategies described on page 88 will help you create a magnetic connection with your listeners that will speed and amplify the transmission of your message.

---

* Detailed instructions on conducting seminars can be found in a companion manual entitled *The Research Essay.*

4. SIMULATIONS

Teachers often use role playing and simulations in the classroom. Simulations develop and reinforce research, oral, and writing skills, while promoting a deeper knowledge and understanding of the topic. Simulations, such as model United Nations or Commonwealth assemblies, trials, elections, and investigative commissions are widely used in schools.

The sample simulation outlined below allows for both maximum class involvement and also for the investigation of a wide range of issues from international, such as global warming to national, such as crime and punishment. In most simulations, the speakers make persuasive speeches: they are trying to persuade the delegates, judges and jurors, voters, and commission members of the validity of their positions.

- Mandate: The Commission will investigate the impact of foreign investment and make recommendations as to whether the government should formulate a more restrictive policy.

- Chairperson welcomes everyone, outlines the mandate and the responsibilities of the Commission and introduces the members of the Commission. (Two minutes)

- Leader of the group favouring restrictions on foreign investment outlines and develops the case against foreign investment. (Five minutes)

- Leader of the group favouring an unrestricted flow of investment outlines and develops the case against restrictions. (Five minutes)

- Questions from the Commission to the members of the two groups probing their positions on the issue. (Twenty minutes)

- Brief caucus for the two groups to prepare their summations. Commission members discuss the responses to their questions. (Four minutes)

- Second speaker for the group favouring an unrestricted flow of investment sums up the case. (Five minutes)

- Second speaker for the group favouring restrictions on investment sums up the case. (Five minutes)

- Chairperson thanks the participants for their contributions and adjourns the proceedings after announcing that the Commission's recommendations will be issued within three days.

- TV host interviews the Chairperson and the two leaders individually for about three minutes each. (Ten minutes)

- Commission members meet over the next few days to decide on their recommendations and to prepare a short written report explaining their decision.

- Newspaper reporter produces an editorial.

- Magazine reporter writes a short article describing the proceedings.

- Teacher makes copies of the Commission's report, the editorial, and the article for the students' notebooks.

- Photographs made available to participants.

- Video of the proceedings replayed for the class.

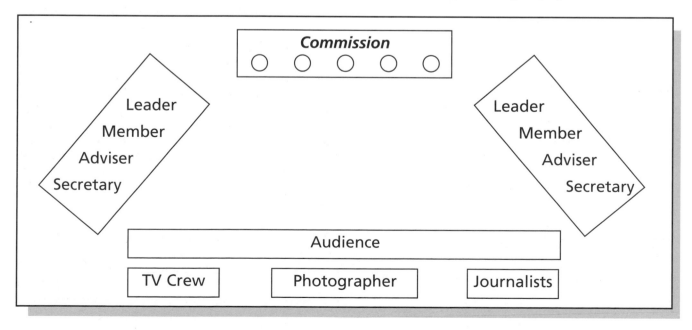

5. DEBATING

Introduction

Debating is used in many subjects to explore different perspectives or points of view on controversial issues. Debating involves most of the skills that you have learned for your research, writing, and public speaking presentations. In addition, the process for preparing debates is similar. There are two major styles of debating: parliamentary and cross examination.

A debate is a formal argument between two opposing teams on a controversial issue. Governed by procedural rules, debating is often described as "organized disagreement." Once a controversial issue has been identified for a debate, the issue, for example, "Nuclear Power" is framed in the form of a proposition or a resolution, such as "Be it resolved that nuclear power should be banned." The resolution is really the response to an underlying question: "Should nuclear power be banned?"

An important issue has been identified and the direction of the assignment defined by a question. In debating, the teacher or the tournament director will decide the response to the question and formulate it as a resolution. The resolution in a debate is equivalent to the thesis statement in an essay.

A well defined resolution on a controversial issue draws a clear line between the pro and con sides and sets the stage for a lively debate. There are three basic types of resolutions in debating: resolutions of fact, value, or policy. These types of resolutions may sometimes overlap, especially policy and value resolutions. BIRT is the acronym used in debating for "Be it resolved that . . ."

Resolutions of fact:

BIRT the Vikings discovered America.

BIRT TV causes more harm than good.

BIRT lower taxes produce a higher incidence of crime.

Resolutions of value:

BIRT individual rights are more important than collective rights.

BIRT genetic engineering should be prohibited.

BIRT automobiles should be banned.

Resolutions of policy:

BIRT security cameras should be banned.

BIRT NAFTA should be expanded to include countries in South America.

BIRT the monarchy should be abolished in Canada.

The Government (or Affirmative team) promotes the resolution and argues that it deserves support. The Opposition (or Negative team) counters the arguments of the Government and raises doubt about the merits of the resolution. Each team is steadfast in defending its position and uses arguments and evidence to convince the judges that their stance on the resolution is the only acceptable one.

The Speaker, or Moderator, chairs the debate and controls the proceedings. The Speaker must be familiar with debating rules and procedures and must remain impartial throughout the debate. The Clerk, or Timekeeper, is responsible for signalling the time remaining in each speech.

Judging is usually undertaken by a panel of three judges, but occasionally the audience may also determine the outcome of a debate. Criteria similar to public speaking are used for judging a debate.

Classroom Debating

The format for the debate described below has been modified for classroom use. It involves both competition and cooperation and promotes the development of skills that will allow you to pursue tournament debating. Although the procedures might appear different, you will discover that the process for preparing and participating in debates is not unfamiliar territory.

Preparation

Let us assume that your social studies teacher has assigned a debate on the topic of "Energy" and has narrowed the focus of the debate to the controversial issue of "Nuclear Power." The response to the question "Should nuclear power be banned?" has been formulated as the resolution "BIRT nuclear power should be banned." The direction of the debate is clearly mapped out.

The two opposing teams will each be led by the Prime Minister and the Leader of the Opposition assisted by two supporting speakers. An additional member on each team will act as an adviser, secretary and backup speaker if one of the speakers is absent. The two leaders will be responsible for organizing their teams, deciding on the order of the speakers, and arranging the research and preparation. **Coordinated teamwork wins debates.** An important part of the preparation is anticipating the arguments of the opposing team and then developing strategies to counter them.

You will notice from the flow chart opposite that the process for preparing a debate is virtually identical to the process for preparing a research report or essay and an informative speech. The Working Outline has been omitted because, like an essay, it is easier to structure your speech once you have completed the research.

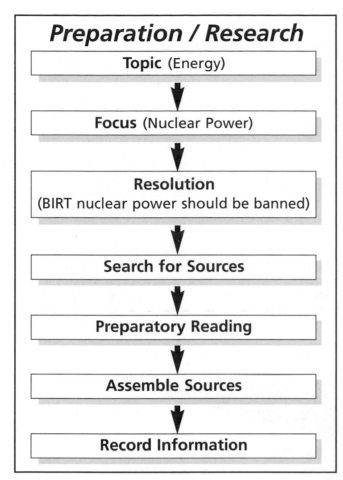

Preparation / Research

Topic (Energy)

↓

Focus (Nuclear Power)

↓

Resolution
(BIRT nuclear power should be banned)

↓

Search for Sources

↓

Preparatory Reading

↓

Assemble Sources

↓

Record Information

Use your skills to build a wide-ranging working bibliography and then undertake the preparatory reading so that you have a thorough understanding of the issue (nuclear power, in our example). Once you have assembled your sources, you are ready to gather the information that you can use to develop compelling arguments in order to prepare a convincing case. Use whichever method you prefer for collecting relevant ideas and information: index cards, notepaper, or a computer.

Just as your research question guided the research for a report, an essay, or an informative speech, so does the resolution guide the research and preparation for a debate. While you are engaged in collecting information for your case, keep a separate piece of notepaper on which you can jot down **counter arguments.** The advisers on each team should concentrate their research on developing an extensive list of counter arguments.

Once the research has been completed, team leaders have to arrange the speaking order for their teams and decide which points each member will emphasize. Team members should then brainstorm the counter arguments that they assembled during the research and be prepared to use these arguments in refuting points raised by the opposing team.

Debating

The order of the proceedings for the debate is sketched out below.

- Speaker welcomes everyone, reads the rules and introduces the two teams.

  (Two minutes)

- Prime Minister states and defines the resolution. Provides brief background information on the resolution and outlines the Government's main arguments.

  (Three minutes)

- Leader of the Opposition outlines the arguments that the Opposition will use to counter the resolution.

  (Three minutes)

- Second Government speaker refutes the Opposition arguments and develops some of the points outlined by the Prime Minister.

  (Three minutes)

- Second Opposition speaker refutes the Government arguments and develops some of the points outlined by the Leader.

  (Three minutes)

- Third Government speaker refutes the Opposition claims and further develops the Government's case.
  (Three minutes)

- Third Opposition speaker refutes the Government claims and further develops the Opposition's arguments.

  (Three minutes)

- Brief caucus for each side to prepare summations.
  (Three minutes)

- Leader of the Opposition sums up.   (Two minutes)

- Prime Minister sums up.   (Two minutes)

- Questions and comments from the audience.
  (Twenty minutes)

- Speaker totals the judges' scores and announces the result.

- Speaker thanks the participants and adjourns the debate.

Teachers may modify the above format by changing the speaking times. For example, comments from the floor may be eliminated to focus on debating skills. It is also possible to involve journalists, photographers, and the TV media in similar roles played in the simulation of the investigative commission.

You will notice that most of the speeches start with a refutation of the previous speaker's points. Debating requires that you listen carefully, take notes while listening, and respond immediately to arguments launched by the opposing side. **You cannot rely on memorized speeches in debating.**

Debating also requires that you speak extemporaneously (or "off the cuff"). If you have prepared the resolution thoroughly and you have a comprehensive list of counter arguments, you will find it much easier to find loopholes in your opponent's speech. Approximately twenty to thirty percent of your speech is devoted to refuting the previous speaker's points.

The second part of your speech is focused on developing the case or position of your team. This segment will have been prepared in advance and written out in Skeleton Outline form on a piece of cardboard or notepaper. Like an essay, you will need to support your arguments with reliable evidence. In concluding your speech, you will summarize your arguments and show how your points fit in to the overall structure of the team's case. If each team has developed a coordinated approach, by the time the third speaker is finished, a well-rounded case will have emerged.

As with other types of speeches, **rehearsing** is an important part of preparing for a debate. Review the tips suggested on page 88 but remember that there are some differences. For example, in debating there is usually more humour, wit, and passion. There is also more drama and gesturing, but excessive theatrics will spoil your speech and may distract the judges. It is your **use of language** that will determine how successfully you have presented your case.

In this classroom debate some of the rules of competitive debating have been modified. For example, the Speaker will not recognize points of order, information, or personal privilege and heckling will not be permitted. Refer to the Glossary on page 107 for an explanation of these terms. The order of the speakers and the seating arrangement have also been changed. Debaters stand when speaking but normally sit when answering questions from the floor. Visual aids (or props) are usually not permitted in debates.

All comments must be directed through the Speaker, who is in charge of the debate. For example, if you are refuting a point made by an opponent, you would state: "Madame (or Mister) Speaker, I would like to point out to the Honourable Member that . . ." In your speeches you refer to team members as "colleagues." Outlined on the next page is a script (or order of the proceedings) that can be used by the Speaker to conduct a debate similar to our example. Never verbally assault or insult an opposing team: **attack issues, not personalities.**

Debating, like public speaking or writing reports and essays, is judged by a range of criteria. Judges use these criteria, such as the debater's knowledge of the resolution and skills of delivery, to determine the outcome of the debate. Classroom debates are usually evaluated by a panel of three judges who may be experienced debaters or teachers. Sometimes all members of the class may be asked to judge a debate. On page 99 you will find a judging form that can be used to evaluate a debate similar to the example just described.

Teachers will often ask the Prime Minister and the Leader of the Opposition to submit separate abstracts and bibliographies as part of the preparation for the debate. An abstract is a synopsis or summary of the case to be presented with the main supporting arguments. The abstract is usually between 200 and 300 words long and for a debate it includes the following sections:

- a brief explanation of the resolution.

- a summary of the case.

- the main supporting arguments.

The bibliography comprises a list of all the sources each team used to prepare their case. The bibliography is set up according to one of the standard styles of documentation explained earlier in this manual. Both the abstract and the bibliography may be assessed by the teacher as part of the evaluation of the debate.

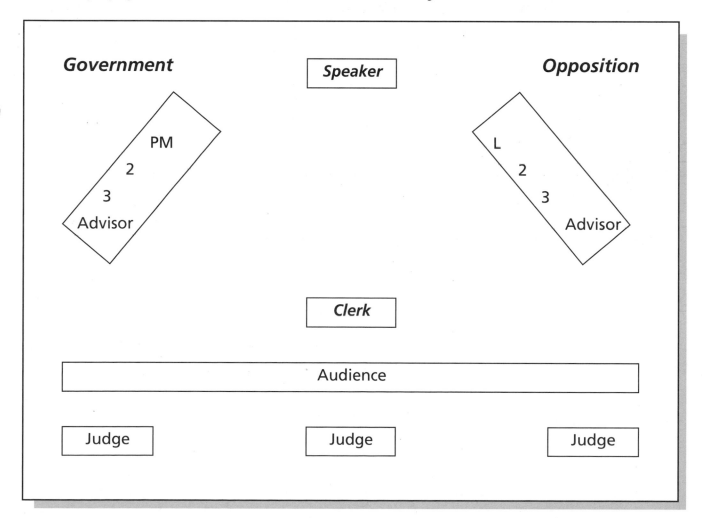

[The Speaker ensures that the names of the members of the Government and the Opposition and the resolution are correctly written on the board. The Speaker chairs the debate using the following script.]

I now call the House to order. Welcome to this classroom debate on the topic of Nuclear Energy. The resolution before the House today is "BIRT nuclear power should be banned."

Debating on the side of the Government are the Prime Minister _____ and Cabinet Ministers _____ and _____ .

Debating on the side of the Opposition are the Leader of the Opposition _____ and Members _____ and _____ .

I, _____ will be the Speaker for this debate and _____ is the Clerk of the House. On behalf of the House, I extend a special welcome to our judges, _____ , _____ , and _____ .

Would the Clerk please demonstrate the signals for timekeeping? (Pause while the Clerk demonstrates the hand signals used for counting down the time remaining in each speech.)

Thank you. No heckling, points of order, personal privilege, or information will be permitted in this debate.

- I now call on the Prime Minister to define the resolution and outline the Government's case for three minutes.

- Thank you. I now call on the Leader of the Opposition to outline the Opposition's arguments against the resolution for three minutes.

- Thank you. I now call upon the second speaker for the Government to refute the Opposition's arguments and to develop the Government's case for three minutes.

- Thank you. I now call upon the second member of the Opposition to refute the Government's arguments and develop the Opposition's case for three minutes.

- Thank you. I now call upon the third speaker for the Government to refute the Opposition's arguments and complete the explanation of the Government's case for three minutes.

- Thank you. I now call upon the third speaker for the Opposition to refute the Government's arguments and to complete the Opposition's case for three minutes.

- There will now be a three minute caucus for each side to prepare its concluding summary.

- We will now hear the final summations for two minutes beginning with the Leader of the Opposition.

- Thank you. The Prime Minister now has two minutes to summarize the Government's case.

- Thank you. I will now entertain questions and comments from the floor for twenty minutes. Please direct your questions through me to a specific speaker. You may also make comments on points raised in the debate.

- Thank you for your questions and comments.

- Would the Clerk please collect the scoresheets from the judges? The Speaker counts the judges' scores and announces the result: I hereby declare that the resolution has been carried / defeated.

- On behalf of the House, I thank the judges and the clerk for their assistance. I congratulate the debaters on their performances and I declare the House adjourned.

DEBATING

Resolution: _____

_____

GOVERNMENT			MEMBERS	OPPOSITION		
PM	2	3		LO	2	3
			Content / Evidence (5)			
			Organization / Clarity (5)			
			Argument / Reasoning (5)			
			Delivery / Presentation (5)			
			Total			

TEAM

	Preparation (10)	
	Refuting Arguments (10)	
	Handling Questions (10)	
	Teamwork (10)	

/ 60   +   / 40   →   / 100

/ 60   +   / 40   →   / 100

TOTAL

Judge _____

Competitive Debating

The classroom debate just described is a hybrid model based on different styles of debating. The purpose of the classroom debate is to introduce students to parliamentary and cross examination debating using a more flexible format. Competitive parliamentary and cross examination debates usually have two speakers on each team and are conducted according to prescribed rules of procedure. While the basic procedure is similar to the classroom debate, much of the advice about preparation, planning, and presentation and the importance of teamwork in classroom debating applies also to competitive debating.

Space does not permit us to print all the rules and regulations for competitive debating. The basic procedures for parliamentary and cross examination debating, the two most popular styles, are outlined in the pages ahead. A glossary of debating terms is also provided. Detailed explanations are available in manuals and websites published and maintained by regional, national, and international debating associations. A selection of websites is listed below.

Bilingual debating provides an opportunity to debate in two languages. Except for minor differences, the rules for bilingual debating are largely the same as those for other forms of debating. For example, at the beginning of the debate, the first speaker explains and defines the terms of the resolution in both languages. In a bilingual parliamentary debate, at least twenty-five percent of the speech must be delivered in one language before the debater switches to the other. In a cross examination debate, the constructive argument is delivered in one language and the summary-rebuttal in the other. Cross examination questions may alternate between the two languages, but must always be answered in the language they were asked. Other than that, switching back and forth between languages is not permitted.

If you enjoyed participating in the classroom debate, consider joining your school debating club. If your school does not have a debating club consider establishing one with the assistance of a teacher. The **research, listening, and speaking skills** that you acquire in debating will stand you in good stead throughout your life.

Alberta Speech and Debate Association	http://www.compusmart.ab.ca/adebate/main.htm
American Parliamentary Debate Association	http://www.apdaweb.org
British Debating	http://www.britishdebate.com
Canadian Student Debating Federation	http://csdf.freeservers.com/core.html
Debate New Brunswick	http://debatenb.freeservers.com
Debating Links	http://www.debating.net/flynn/deblinks.htm
Fédération canadienne des débats d'étudiants	http://www.commelair.com/fcde
The Fulford League	http://www.fulford.org
International Independent Schools Public Speaking League	http://www.iispsl.org
Japan Parliamentary Debate Web Resource	http://www.asahi-net.or.jp/~cj3m-lbky/parlidebate.html
Manitoba Speech and Debate Association	http://www.sjr.mb.ca/debate
National Junior High Debating Championships	http://www.sjr.mb.ca/debate/jrnatlcontents.htm
National Public Speaking Championships	http://www.sjr.mb.ca/debate/natlPSgeneral.htm
National Senior High Debating Championships	http://www.sjr.mb.ca/debate/srnatlcontents.htm
Ontario Student Debating Union	http://www.osdu.oise.utoronto.ca
Saskatchewan Elocution and Debate Association	http://www.saskdebate.com

Parliamentary Debating

Parliamentary debating is the most popular form of debating. You may encounter some minor differences in the formats for competitive parliamentary debating. For example, the time per speaker and the number of debaters on each team can vary. The format described below is widely used in debating tournaments. Once you have mastered the basic skills of debating, you will easily be able to adjust to variations in debating formats.

Prime Minister	3 minutes
First Opposition Speaker	5 minutes
Second Government Speaker	5 minutes
Leader of the Opposition	5 minutes
Prime Minister	2 minutes

You will notice that the Prime Minister speaks first and last but the total time does not exceed the other speakers. Normally, total speaking times will vary between five and eight minutes in competitive debating. The roles and responsibilities of speakers in a parliamentary debate involving two-person teams are described below. Except for minor differences, the process is similar to the classroom debate, allowing you to make an easy transition to competitive debating.

• The **Prime Minister** explains the resolution and defines the key terms. (The Opposition will exploit any confusion arising from a vaguely defined resolution.) The Prime Minister then outlines the Government's case in promoting the resolution, mentioning the main supporting arguments and developing at least one of them.

• The **First Opposition Speaker** refutes the arguments presented by the Prime Minister and outlines the Opposition's position on the resolution. Then the First Opposition Speaker advances the Opposition's case by developing at least one of their main points.

• The **Second Government Speaker** refutes the Opposition's attack on the Government's case. The Second Government speaker then completes the case for the Government by explaining the remaining points.

• The **Leader of the Opposition** refutes the previous speaker's points and attempts to discredit the Government's case. The Leader presents the final constructive arguments for the Opposition and then sums up by giving an overview of the Opposition's case.

• The **Prime Minister** concludes the debate by refuting the claims of the Opposition and restating and summarizing the Government's case. No new information or arguments are permitted in this speech.

Heckling and points of order, personal privilege, and, sometimes, information are an integral part of competitive parliamentary debating. Develop your skills by learning how to use these strategies but do not interrupt a debate too frequently for trivial reasons. Repeated interruptions will not endear you to the judges. Stand when you speak or raise one of the three types of points mentioned above, but remain seated when heckling.

The Speaker is in charge of a parliamentary debate and uses a script similar to the script in the classroom debate. As in the classroom debate, all speeches and comments are addressed to and through the Speaker. Competitive debating requires an experienced Speaker because of the detailed rules and the challenges of dealing with heckling and points of order, personal privilege, and information.

Judging in competitive debating is also similar to the classroom debate. Judges focus on three main areas in competitive debating: the **content** and **delivery** of the speeches and debating **skills.** The specific criteria for evaluating debates, however, are similar to those used in the classroom debate, as you will notice from the sample form on the next page. Tournament directors may sometimes exclude "Team work" as a criterion. In such a case, the "Team work" box on page 102 can be left blank. The evaluation form on page 103 allows for judges to comment on individual debaters.

PARLIAMENTARY DEBATING

Resolution: _____

_____

TEAM / SCHOOL: _____   **TEAM / SCHOOL:** _____

GOVERNMENT PM	2		OPPOSITION 1	LO
		Content / Evidence ( )		
		Organization / Clarity ( )		
		Argument / Reasoning ( )		
		Refutation / Rebuttal ( )		
		Delivery / Presentation ( )		
		Procedure / Skills ( )		
		TOTAL		

+

+

TEAM WORK

TOTAL

Judge _____

DEBATING

Debater: _____   Role: _____

Resolution: _____

_____

Content / Evidence	⬜
Organization / Clarity	⬜
Argument / Reasoning	⬜
Refutation / Rebuttal	⬜
Delivery / Presentation	⬜
Procedure / Skills	⬜
TOTAL	⬜

Comments: _____

_____

_____

_____

_____

Judge: _____

Cross Examination Debating

What are the differences between parliamentary and cross examination debating? In cross examination debating:

- The Government is called the Affirmative team and the Opposition is referred to as the Negative team.

- The Prime Minister is known as the First Affirmative speaker and the Second Government speaker as the Second Affirmative speaker. The Opposition speakers are referred to as the First and Second Negative speakers.

- Resolutions in a parliamentary debate are usually policy resolutions, while in cross examination debating they tend to be resolutions of value.

- The Speaker is termed the Moderator.

- No points of order, personal privilege, and information or heckling are permitted.

- Opponents are addressed by title, such as the "First Affirmative Speaker," or by name, such as "Ms . . ." or "Mr . . ." The audience is referred to as "Ladies and Gentlemen."

- Each debater is questioned by an opponent after speaking.

- The ability of debaters to ask and answer questions is also judged.

What are the similarities between parliamentary and cross examination debating?

- The First Affirmative Speaker defines the resolution and outlines the arguments that will be used to promote it.

- The First Negative Speaker outlines the approach that will be used to counter the resolution.

- Preparation, planning, and teamwork are important.

- Like writers of essays and reports, debaters must give their speeches the coherence and clarity of a laser beam, not the chaotic brilliance of a fireworks display.

- The Affirmative team speaks first and last.

- Debaters must analyze the opposing arguments, identify the weaknesses and pursue them.

- Visual aids and props are not permitted.

- The Moderator, like the Speaker, is in charge and follows a similar script.

- The seating positions for the speakers are the same.

- Judges base their decisions on similar criteria.

Like parliamentary debating, there are minor variations in the format for cross examination debating. For example, the speaking order, time per speaker, and the number of debaters on each team can vary. The format outlined below is widely used in competitive debating. Sometimes all four speakers will each be required to deliver a final summary rebuttal.

First Affirmative Speaker	5 minutes
Cross examined by Second Negative Speaker	3 minutes
First Negative Speaker	5 minutes
Cross examined by First Affirmative Speaker	3 minutes
Second Affirmative Speaker	5 minutes
Cross examined by First Negative Speaker	3 minutes
Second Negative Speaker	5 minutes
Cross examined by Second Affirmative Speaker	3 minutes
Prepare final summations	2-3 minutes
First Negative Speaker delivers summary rebuttal	3 minutes
First Affirmative Speaker delivers summary rebuttal	3 minutes

The skills that you have acquired for researching and writing reports and essays, presenting speeches and viewpoints, and participating in simulations and classroom debates, will have prepared you well for competitive debating. "Practice makes perfect" is as true of debating as any other activity.

Advice for examiners:

- Be prepared.
- Ask precise, clear questions.
- Prepare some questions in advance.
- Focus the questions on the opposition's arguments.
- Do not harass, insult or argue with a witness.
- Probe for weaknesses and try to draw a witness into acknowledging shortcomings in their case.
- Be courteous and polite.
- Keep the witness on track.
- Stay in control.
- Avoid being overly dramatic.
- You may only question; you may not comment.
- Use admissions and other information gained from the examination in later rebuttals and summaries.

Advice for witnesses:

- Be prepared.
- Stay calm; do not get emotional.
- Listen carefully to the questions.
- Give concise, honest answers.
- Do not stall or evade answers.
- Do not argue.
- Be cooperative and polite.
- Do not be flippant.
- Ask for clarification if a question is confusing.
- Be aware of where the examiner may be trying to lead you.
- Attempt to convince the audience and the judges, not the examiner.
- Use information that emerges during the examination in later rebuttals and summaries.

Moderator's Script

The debate will come to order. The resolution before us today is _____ _____ .

Speaking in favour of the resolution are the First Affirmative _____ and the Second Affirmative _____ .

Speaking against the resolution are the First Negative _____ and the Second Negative _____ .

I, _____ , am your Moderator and the Timekeeper is _____ .

Each debater will deliver a five-minute speech, after which he or she will be cross examined by an opponent for three minutes. The first speaker on each side will give a three-minute summary rebuttal. The Timekeeper will indicate how much time has elapsed. Heckling and points of order, information, and privilege are not allowed.

- I now call upon the First Affirmative to deliver his/her speech, after which he/she will be questioned by the Second Negative.
- I thank the First Affirmative and call upon the First Negative to speak, after which he/she will be questioned by the First Affirmative.
- I thank the First Negative and call upon the Second Affirmative who will be questioned by the First Negative.
- I thank the Second Affirmative and call upon the Second Negative who will be questioned by the Second Affirmative.
- There will now be a two minute pause for members to finalize their summations.
- I call upon the First Negative to deliver the final summary rebuttal for the Negative side, reminding him/her that no new evidence may be introduced.
- I call upon the First Affirmative to deliver the final summary rebuttal for the Affirmative side, again cautioning against the introduction of any new evidence.
- I congratulate the debaters on their speeches.
- I thank the Judges and the Timekeeper for their assistance and declare the debate adjourned.

[Judges hand their completed ballots to the Timekeeper and are then invited to make brief comments on the debate. The results are usually announced later.]

CROSS EXAMINATION DEBATING

Resolution: _____

_____

TEAM / SCHOOL: **TEAM / SCHOOL:**

AFFIRMATIVE 1	2		NEGATIVE 1	2
		Content / Evidence ( )		
		Organization / Clarity ( )		
		Argument / Reasoning ( )		
		Refutation / Rebuttal ( )		
		Delivery / Presentation ( )		
		Examining ( )		
		Witness ( )		
		TOTAL		

+   +

TEAM WORK

TOTAL

Judge _____

Glossary

Academic:	A variation of parliamentary style debating which has points of information but no points of order or personal privilege.
Affirmative:	The team defending the resolution in cross examination debating.
Ballot:	Scoresheet completed by the judges during the debate.
BIRT:	Acronym for "Be It Resolved That" which prefaces the resolution.
Burden of Proof:	Rests on the Government side to prove the need for and the feasibility of the affirmative case.
Case:	The overall argument for the affirmative or negative side of the debate including all its evidence, claims and reasons.
Clash:	When argument and counter-argument meet head-on in direct refutation and rebuttal. The crux of good debating.
Constructive Speech:	The debater's presentation of case-points.
Cross Examination:	Style of debating which has a direct question and answer period for each debater, but no heckling, points of order or personal privilege.
Deconstruction:	The refutation or attack on the opponent's case.
Discussion:	A variation of cross examination style of debating which replaces the cross examination period with a discussion period.
Factual Resolution:	A type of debate topic which implies that a statement is accurate or true.
Government:	The term for the affirmative team in parliamentary debating.
Heckle:	A short, witty remark made by a debater during an opponent's speech in parliamentary debating.
Negative Team:	The team arguing against the resolution in cross examination debating.
Opposition:	The term for the negative team in parliamentary debating.
Parliamentary:	The style of debating which proposes and argues bills, uses parliamentary terminology and allows heckling, points of order and points of personal privilege.
Point of Information:	Initiated by a debater raising his/her hand to request further information on a point or clarification of a point.
Point of Order:	When a rule is broken in parliamentary debating, a debater stands and says: "I rise on a point of order, Madam Speaker." Perhaps new evidence was introduced in the Prime Minister's final rebuttal or the definition of the resolution was unacceptable. The Speaker responds with either "That point is well taken" or " That point is not well taken" and the debate resumes.
Point of Privilege:	When a debater has been insulted or misquoted in parliamentary debating. The procedure is the same as for the Point of Order.
Policy Resolution:	A type of debate topic which proposes the need for a change in Government policy.
Reasonable Doubt:	Attempts by the negative team to emphasize weaknesses in the affirmative's case.
Rebuttal:	The reconstruction and rebuilding of the argument after an attack by your opponent.
Refutation:	The attack on your opponent's argument.
Resolution:	The topic of the debate expressed as a statement and prefaced with BIRT.
Signposting:	Numbering and labeling the main points in your argument to make them easy for you and your audience to identify and remember. For example, your first point might be an economic one.
Value Resolution:	A type of debate topic that focuses on what is right or good.

INTERNATIONAL SCHOOLS' COMPETITION

If you would like to establish public speaking clubs in your school, you may be interested to read about the range of activities that comprise the annual International Independent Schools Public Speaking Competition. Visit their website at: <http://www.iispsl.org>

Impromptu Speaking

Each speaker draws three topics which may be quotations, phrases, or a single word. Speakers select one topic and have two minutes to prepare their comments. Each participant must speak for three to five minutes. Penalties are applied to speeches outside the time limit.

Extemporaneous Speaking

Each speaker draws three topics on major national and international news stories. The topics are phrased in the form of questions. Speakers select one topic and they have thirty minutes to prepare their speeches. Each participant must speak for three to five minutes, referring to notes if necessary. Penalties are applied to speeches outside the time limit.

Interpretive Reading

Each participant reads, not recites, a passage of published prose or poetry for a period of seven to thirteen minutes. The speaker prepares a brief introduction of less than a minute about the author and the work and the reason for selecting it. Emphasis is on the reader's voice and interpretation of the material and not on theatrical performance.

Dramatic Interpretation

This is a memorized presentation selected from published plays with literary merit. A simple costume and one prop are permitted but they are not mandatory. The time limit of five to twelve minutes includes a brief introduction of less than a minute about the material.

Newscast

Each participant is given a copy of a newspaper. After thirty minutes preparation, the speaker must deliver a four minute radio broadcast. Information must be drawn from the newspaper. Judging is based on selection of news, clarity of presentation, originality, use of voice, and adherence to time. Judges may sit with their backs to the "newscasters" or alternatively, the newscast may be delivered from behind a curtain.

After-Dinner Speaking

Each speaker delivers an informative and entertaining address to an imaginary audience that must be identified at the start of the speech. Participants speak for five minutes with minimal reference to notes and no use of props.

Persuasive Speaking

This is a prepared speech where the speaker identifies a problem and then proposes solutions. Persuasion is the key element in this presentation. Speeches are from seven to thirteen minutes in length with minimal reference to notes.

Parliamentary Debating

Teams consist of two debaters who have been paired randomly. Topics are presented thirty minutes before the debate starts. One team chooses the topic and the other team selects which side (Government or Opposition) it will take. The debate is conducted according to standard parliamentary procedure.

Cross Examination Debating

This debate is on a prepared topic and school-based teams debate both sides of the topic. Each team consists of two debaters and the debate is conducted according to the standard rules of cross examination debating.

8 Conclusion

This guide has taken you step by step through the process of researching and presenting reports, essays, and speeches. This is the end of this stage of your journey. You have been provided with the basic skills to help you complete your assignments successfully.

As you research and write your reports and essays and prepare your speeches, you will be setting your own directions and plotting your own routes. With proper provisions and equipment, practice and experience, you will soon become an expert explorer, and, unlike a tourist wandering aimlessly without even a compass for direction, you will never find yourself lost in the woods.

Moreover, by developing your skills and shaping your own personal pathway, you will be able to reach your destination in less time with less effort and enjoy the trip more. Although resources and technology will change and evolve, you will always be able to modify your basic pathway and adjust it for any changes.

Every report and essay that you write and every speech that you prepare is a journey of exploration and discovery. You will learn about yourself, you will learn about the topic, and you will learn skills ranging from cooperating with other students to library research techniques. Take the knowledge and the skills with you and make each journey more fulfilling than the last.

There are still countless questions waiting to be asked and countless problems to investigate. Many exciting journeys lie ahead.

After your project has been handed back to you . . .

- Read your teacher's comments carefully.

- Discuss any comments that are unclear with your teacher.

- Read the best projects in each class and compare them with yours.

- Write a personal critique of each project.

- Make a list of weaknesses to address in your next project.

- Keep all your assignments to mark your progress.

1. ILLUSTRATIONS

There are two major types of illustrations: tables and figures. Tables contain statistical data, while figures consist of photographs, maps, drawings, graphs, diagrams, charts, painting, and pictures. Software, such as spreadsheets or graphics programs, allows you to do most illustrations on a computer. Computers also allow you to scan images and information and to merge and embed illustrations in the text. If computer facilities are not available, tables and figures can still be prepared by hand. Aim for clarity and simplicity when laying out your illustrations. Demonstrated on the following pages are some of the more commonly used illustrations.

1. Tables

Statistical tables are either set at the relevant place in the text or placed in the appendix. Each table is assigned a concise title and a number. The source of the information must also be given unless the data are generated from your own fieldwork. The data in each table must be carefully explained in the text of a report or clearly linked to the development of the thesis in an essay. Do not include tables simply to fill space. Keep your tables simple and include only the essential details. An example of a table is shown below.

2. Figures

Like tables, figures are placed either in the body or in the appendix. The title is placed below the figure and accompanied by the source of the information. Figures are numbered consecutively throughout the assignment. Any symbols must be explained in a legend and placed within the figure. Always ask yourself whether a figure is necessary and whether it actually illustrates a point. A variety of figures are illustrated on the following pages. Ensure that you use the most appropriate charts and graphs to illustrate statistical information.

Table 1. Elevations, Areas, and Depth of the Great Lakes

Lake	Elevation (m)	Length (km)	Breadth (km)	Maximum depth (m)	Total area (km²)
Superior	184	563	257	405	82 100
Michigan	176	494	190	281	57 800
Huron	177	332	295	229	59 600
Erie	174	338	92	64	25 700
Ontario	75	311	85	244	18 960

Source: *Canada Year Book 2001* (Ottawa: Statistics Canada, 2001), 39.

Maps

Fig. 1. The Great Lakes.

Organizational Charts

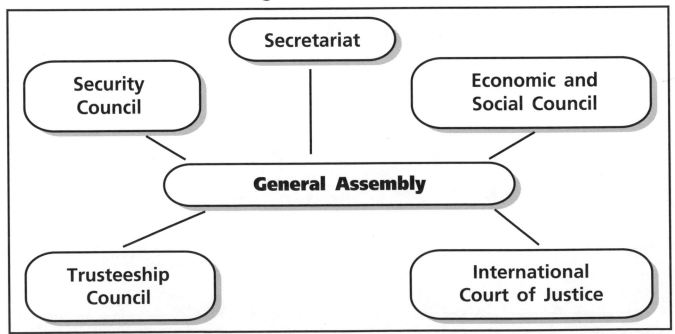

Fig. 2. The United Nations System.

Line Graphs

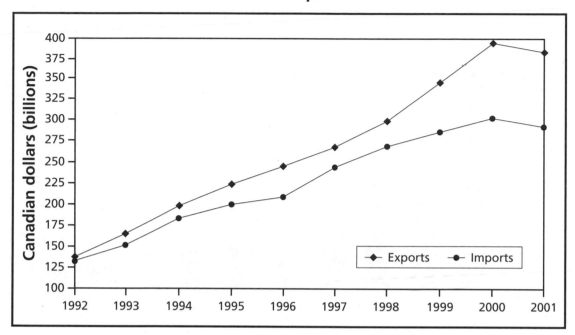

Fig. 3. Canada's Trade with the United States.
Source: Canada's Balance of International Payments, 4th Quarter 2001, Statistics Canada.

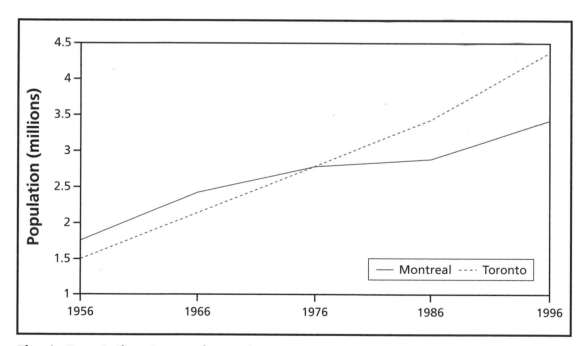

Fig. 4. Population Comparison of Toronto and Montreal.
Source: John R. Colombo, ed., *The Canadian Global Almanac* (Toronto: Macmillan, 1998), 54.

Bar / Column Charts

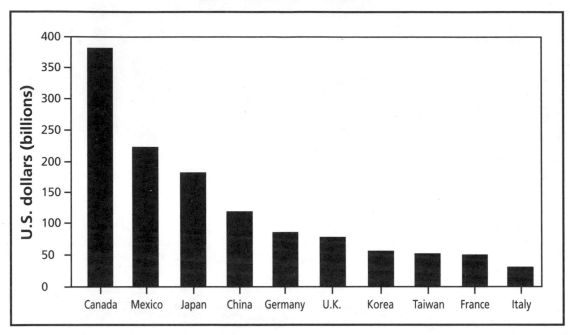

Fig. 5. United States' Main Trading Partners, 2001.
Source: U.S. Department of Commerce, Bureau of the Census, *Top Ten Countries with which the U.S. Trades* (December 2001). <http://www.census.gov/foreign-trade/top/dst/current/balance.html> (10 January 2002).

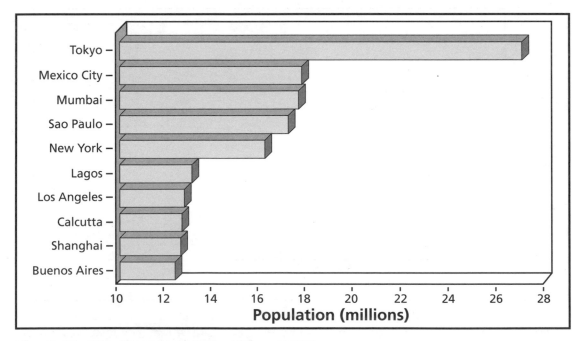

Fig. 6. World's Most Populous Cities, 2000.
Source: *The World Almanac and Book of Facts* (New York: World Almanac Books, 2002), 869.

Circle / Pie Charts

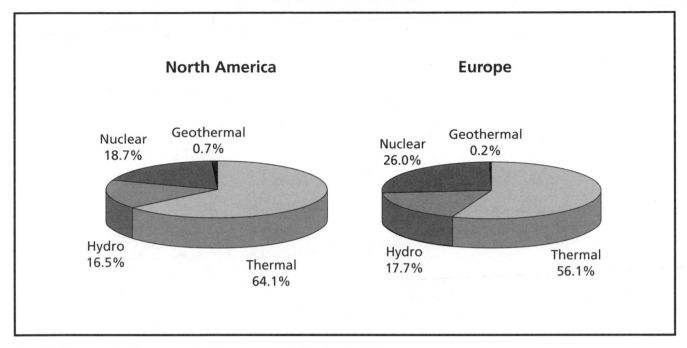

North America

Nuclear
18.7%

Geothermal
0.7%

Hydro
16.5%

Thermal
64.1%

Europe

Nuclear
26.0%

Geothermal
0.2%

Hydro
17.7%

Thermal
56.1%

Fig. 7. Sources of Energy in Europe and North America.
Source: *1995 Energy Statistics Yearbook* (New York: United Nations, 1997), 432 and 448.

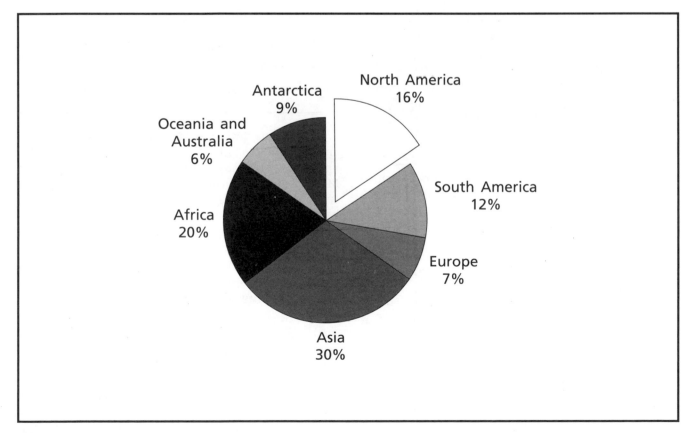

North America
16%

Antarctica
9%

Oceania and
Australia
6%

Africa
20%

Asia
30%

Europe
7%

South America
12%

Fig. 8. Continents by Area.
Source: *The World Almanac and Book of Facts* (Mahwah, NJ: K-111 Reference Corp., 1997), 838.

2. MLA DOCUMENTATION

You have been introduced to the three major documentation styles: the parenthetical APA (American Psychological Association) and MLA (Modern Language Association) systems and the footnote/endnote system based on *The Chicago Manual of Style*. Remember that documentation involves two key elements:

- The **citation** is either a parenthetical reference or a superscript number in the text of the essay or report identifying the source of important information.

- The **list of sources** is placed at the end of the essay or report and provides publication details of the in-text citations and it may also include other sources that proved useful in completing the assignment.

The MLA system is widely used in preparing assignments on literary works. The sample essays on "Long, Long after School" and *Animal Farm* used the MLA system but because they were based on a single primary text, it was only necessary to cite the page number in parentheses. However, if you are writing a report or an essay on a literary topic that involves research in other primary and/or secondary sources, you must know how to cite all the sources according to MLA style.

Both APA and MLA are parenthetical documentation systems. The major difference is that APA requires the date of publication to accompany the author's name (or the title) in the citation, whereas MLA only requires the author's name (or the title) and the page reference for the information. Compare the excerpt below in MLA style from an essay on Alice Munro with the APA example on page 18.

> Stories by this so-called "antiquarian miniaturist" (Fawcett 9) appear in a variety of magazines designed for sophisticated readers. Munro's impeccable technique, her "postmodern view of language" (Perkin 5), is one reason for the international interest in her fiction; she is a master of compression, time-shifting, and subtle metaphor.

The in-text citations have to be linked to a list of sources at the end of the essay or report. However, if you compare pages 20–21 with pages 117–18 you will notice that the details in the APA and MLA source lists are entered differently. It is essential that you link the citation procedure with the corresponding procedure for listing the sources at the end of the assignment. You must not, for example, use MLA in-text citations with an APA reference list or Chicago/Turabian numbered notes with an MLA bibliography.

In writing research projects on literary topics, it is common for teachers to require a final list of sources that includes **just the works cited** in the report or essay. The sample bibliography for the Alice Munro essay below illustrates a "Works Cited" in MLA style. If your teacher requires a list of sources that includes **all the sources** that proved useful in completing the assignment, title it "Bibliography" or "Works Consulted."

Works Cited

Blodgett, E.D. *Alice Munro.* Boston: Twayne, 1988.

Fawcett, Brian. "Me and My Gang." *Books in Canada* Dec. 1991: 8-9.

Munro, Alice. *The Moons of Jupiter.* Markham, ON: Penguin, 1983.

- - -. *The Progress of Love.* Toronto: McClelland and Stewart, 1986.

Perkins, Russell. Letter. *Books in Canada* Mar. 1992: 5.

Woodcock, George. "The Secrets of Her Success." *Quill & Quire* 60 (1994): 25. *Literature Resource Center.* Ottawa Public Library. 2 Aug. 2002 <http://galenet.galegroup.com/servlet/LitRC>.

MLA style is similar to APA and Chicago/Turabian in entering the first line flush with the left margin and leaving a double space between each source. However, MLA, unlike the other styles, requires that a double space also be left between lines when a source extends beyond one line, as shown above.[15]

When listing two or more books by the same author, enter the name for the first entry only. For the next and successive entries, type three hyphens followed by a period. Then enter the title and publication details. Sources are entered in alphabetical order by title. See the Munro examples above.

On the following two pages you will find the same sample sources that were listed earlier in APA and Chicago/Turabian styles, arranged according to MLA guidelines. However, the entries have been single-spaced, not double-spaced as explained above, to conserve space. All titles have been italicized in these examples. If you are using a word processor, titles should be italicized. In handwritten or typed essays, titles are underlined.

Book

One Author

Bonvillain, Nancy. *The Huron.* New York: Chelsea House, 1989.

Two Authors

Strunk, William, Jr., and E.B. White. *The Elements of Style.* New York: Macmillan, 1979.

Multiple Authors

Colborn, Theodora, et al. Great Lakes, Great Legacy? Washington: The Conservation Foundation, 1990.

Editor

Krueger, Anne, ed. *The WTO as an International Organization.* Chicago: U of Chicago P, 1998.

No Author

The Great Lakes: An Environmental Atlas and Resource Book. Chicago: United States Environmental Protection Agency and Toronto: Environment Canada, 1995.

Corporate Author

American Psychological Association. *Publication Manual.* 5th ed. Washington, DC: American Psychological Association, 2001.

Later Edition

Zinsser, William. *On Writing Well.* 6th ed. New York: HarperCollins, 1998.

Magazine

Leahy, Stephen. "Lake Erie's small but toxic killers." *Maclean's* 16 Dec. 2001: 114.

Journal

Zorpette, G. "Mussel Mayhem." *Scientific American* 275 (1996): 22-23.

Newspaper

Binder, David. "Great Lakes face endless battle with marine invaders." *New York Times* 11 July 2000: F4.

Encyclopedia

Iverson, P. "Navajo." *Encyclopedia Americana.* 3rd ed. 2000.

Yearbook

Yapko, Michael, D. "Repressed Memories: Special Report." *Britannica Book of the Year 1995.* Chicago: Encyclopedia Britannica, 1996.

Video recording

The Civil War. Dir. Ken Burns. Videocassette. PBS, 1994.

Government Report

International Joint Commission. *Protection of the Waters of the Great Lakes.* Ottawa, ON and Washington, DC: International Joint Commission, 2000.

Interview

Smales, Simon. Personal interview. 5 June 2000.

Film

Dances with Wolves. Dir. Kevin Costner. TIG and Orion,1990.

Radio and Television Program

The Great Egyptians. Prod. P. Spry-Leverton. Narr. B. Brier. Learning Channel, 27 Aug. 1998.

Art

Picasso, Pablo. *Still Life with Chair-Caning.* 1912. Musee Picasso, Paris.

Map

Physical United States. Map. Washington, DC: National Geographic, 2000.

CD-ROM / DVD

Discover the Great Lakes: The Ecosystem of the Great Lakes-St. Lawrence. CD-ROM. Ottawa: Environment Canada, 1997.

Art

da Vinci, Leonardo. *The Mona Lisa.* 1506. Louvre, Paris. 1 Dec. 2002 <http://www.louvre.fr/anglais/collec/peint/inv0779/peint_f.htm>.

Book

Dickens, Charles. *Great Expectations.* 1861. 29 Nov. 2002 <http://www.bibliomania.com/0/0/19/frameset.html>.

Email

Sandler, Judy. "Re: Zebra mussels." Email to Susan Conway. 6 July 2002.

Encyclopedia

Farr, D.M.L. "The Alaska Boundary Dispute." *The Canadian Encyclopedia.* 2002. 25 Oct. 2002 <http://www.thecanadianencyclopedia.com/index.cfm> Search: "Alaska Boundary Dispute."

General Website

Archaeological Survey of Canada. *The Draper Site.* 20 July 2001. 10 Sept. 2002 <http://www.civilization.ca/cmc/archeo/oracles/draper/drape.htm>.

Journal

Menichetti, David. "German Policy in Occupied Belgium, 1914-1918." *Essays in History* 39. (1997). 9 Feb. 2002 <http://etext.lib.virginia.edu/journals/EH/EH39/menich39.html>.

Magazine

Tal, Guy. "Learning to Photograph the Landscape." *Nature Photographers Online Magazine* Sept. 2002. 27 Nov. 2002 <http://www.naturephotographers.net/articles0902/gt0902-1.html>.

Map

The Axis Powers, 1942. Map.13 Sept. 2002 <http://www.indstate.edu/gga/gga_cart/78927.jpg>.

Newspaper

Schmadeke, Steve. "Fierce flies are deployed to fight Florida fire ants." *Naples Daily News* 27 Nov. 2002. 1 Dec. 2002 <http://www.naplesnews.com/02/11/naples/d865261a.htm>.

Photograph

Neville Chamberlain with Adolf Hitler. 1997. Photograph. Simon Wiesenthal Center. 22 June 2002 <http://motlc.wiesenthal.com/gallery/pg18/pg7/pg18722.html>.

Professional Website

Crouse, Maurice. *Citing Electronic Information in History Papers.* 18 Oct. 2002. 18 Dec. 2002 <http://www.people.memphis.edu/~mcrouse/elcite.html>.

Question and Answer Database

The Chicago Manual of Style. *FAQ (and not so FAQ).* 2002. 6 Dec. 2002 <http://www.press.uchicago.edu/Misc/Chicago/cmosfaq/>.

Radio / Television

O'Neill, Mark. "Chinese Traditional Medicines." *Quirks and Quarks.* CBC Radio, Toronto. 23 May 1998. 5 Jan. 2001 <http://www.radio.cbc.ca/programs/quirks/realaud/may2398.ra>.

Subscription Database

Woodcock, George. "The Secrets of Her Success." *Quill & Quire* 60 (1994): 25. *Literature Resource Center.* Ottawa Public Library. 2 Aug. 2002 <http://galenet.galegroup.com/servlet/LitRC>.

Glossary

Abstract A synopsis of your report or essay that highlights the main points. It is between 100 and 300 words in length and is placed immediately after the title page.

Analysis Examining and dissecting the text or the research material closely in accordance with the question or purpose of the assignment, then identifying important ideas and elements and isolating the relevant details.

Annotated bibliography A list of sources accompanied by comments on the merits of each source.

APA documentation The documentation style of the American Psychological Association. The source is identified by a parenthetical citation containing the author's name, date of publication of the work, and the page reference.

Argument See **Thesis.**

Bias The intentional and prejudicial selection of information to support a predetermined point of view.

Bibliography Literally a list of books used as sources for an essay or a report. Now commonly used to refer to all types of sources found useful in completing a research assignment.

Citation A brief reference in the text of the report or essay identifying the source of a quotation, idea, or information. Either a parenthetical reference or a superscript number is used.

Classify Organize ideas and information into groups, categories, or classes of similar features.

Compare Show the connection or relationship between different individuals, events, or issues by focusing on the similarities and/or differences.

Contrast Show the connection or relationship between different individuals, events, or issues by focusing on the differences only.

Creative thinking Brainstorming new ideas and generating imaginative insights. Thinking creatively also involves exploring other approaches to problems and issues, as well as classifying ideas and information.[16]

Critical thinking Evaluating existing information and knowledge. Thinking critically involves skills, such as detecting bias and determining the reliability and relevance of evidence.[17]

Documentation The process of citing and listing the sources of quotations, important information, and paraphrased ideas used in your project.

Endnotes A method of documentation where the source is indicated by a superscript number in the text and the details of the source are provided at the end of the essay or report.

Essay A formal piece of writing developed around a central thesis or argument which is supported by evidence, ideas, and reasons.

Evaluate Examine and judge the strengths and weaknesses of a source, argument, or speech according to specified criteria.

Explain A term that can either mean to clarify and make something "plain," such as "Explain the Potlatch ceremony of the West Coast indigenous people." Alternatively, it may require developing a point of view or an argument, such as "Explain the collapse of the Atlantic fishing industry." The former requires a report response; the latter is an essay.

Explanatory note Additional information that, while relevant to the report or essay, may detract from the development of the theme or thesis if inserted directly into the text. This information is usually placed in a footnote, but it can also be set as an endnote.

Exploratory reading The initial reading undertaken to explore a topic for an assignment and to isolate the issues, elements, aspects, and themes suitable for further study and investigation.

Expository writing A form of writing that explains, informs, and clarifies, such as a report.

Figures Illustrations, such as photographs, maps, pictures, charts, diagrams, and drawings.

Footnotes A numbered documentation system where the details of the source are provided at the foot (bottom) of the page.

Genres Major categories of literary works, such as novels, short stories, plays, and poetry.

Hypothesis A provisional proposition or tentative theory in response to a research question, usually used to launch scientific experiments. It is less certain and conclusive than a thesis.

MLA documentation The parenthetical documentation style of the Modern Language Association. MLA style is widely used in language and literature.

Online sources Electronic or digital sources available through the Internet.

Paraphrase Describing a passage from a source or an author's idea in your own words.

Parenthetical documentation A method of documentation where the source is identified in parentheses (brackets) in the text of the report or essay. APA and MLA are the two most common parenthetical systems.

Plagiarism The use of someone else's ideas or work without acknowledgment.

Point of view See Thesis.

Preliminary research The initial stages of the research prior to "Recording Information." The preliminary research lays the groundwork for analyzing and recording the relevant information.

Preparatory reading Background reading about the focus of the assignment once the purpose or question has been formulated. The purpose or question provides direction for the preparatory reading.

Pre-writing A term used in writing about literary topics to describe the preparatory and analytical stages of an assignment prior to composing the report or essay.

Primary source A first-hand account by someone observing an event. It is original material that has not been interpreted by another person.

Project A general term covering a variety of independent or group assignments. Projects can be as varied as research papers, oral presentations, and scrapbooks, and cover both essays and reports.

References A list of sources in alphabetical order used to prepare an essay or a report.

Report The presentation of factual information to inform, explain, clarify, or describe. A report develops a theme but not an opinion, point of view, or thesis.

Research paper An investigation of a problem or issue based on primary and/or secondary sources and the development and substantiation of a thesis or argument. A research paper may sometimes be an expository report.

Research The process of investigating a problem by gathering and analyzing information from primary and/or secondary sources. The research process is guided by a purpose in the form of a question or hypothesis.

Secondary source Information obtained second-hand. It is another person's interpretation of the primary material, usually presented as an argument or point of view.

Seminar An oral presentation of a thesis or point of view followed by a discussion, usually conducted in a group of approximately ten people.

Style The manner in which you express yourself in written language. It is the individual imprint that you leave on your writing. Systems for documenting sources are also frequently referred to as "styles."

Subjectivity Our individual view of the world shaped by the experience of our upbringing. It influences our approach to researching and writing reports and essays.

Summarize Reduce information to its essential details in your own words.

Synthesis The process of structuring and composing your answer or thesis. Analysis is one side of the coin, synthesis is the other side.

Table An illustration containing columns of statistical data.

Term paper See Research paper.

Tertiary source Reference works, such as encyclopedias and yearbooks.

Theme A theme is the response to the research question of a report. It is the central or controlling idea of a report, as opposed to the thesis of an essay. It can also be the central idea of a work of literature.

Thesis The point of view, opinion, or argument around which your essay is built.

Thesis statement A concise statement of your thesis, usually placed at the end of the introduction. The thesis statement is your response to the research question (or the conclusions that you reached) summed up concisely in one or two sentences – it is not the question itself.

Notes

1. Kate L. Turabian, *Student's Guide for Writing College Papers,* 3rd ed. (Chicago: University of Chicago Press, 1976), 31.

2. Alden Todd, *Finding Facts Fast* (Berkeley: Ten Speed Press, 1979), 10.

3. Lucile V. Payne, *The Lively Art of Writing* (Chicago: Follett,1965), 19.

4. Harry F. Wolcott, *Writing up Qualitative Research,* Qualitative Research Methods Series, vol.20 (Newbury Park, CA: Sage Publications, 1990), 69.

5. Edward de Bono, *CORT 1: Teachers' Notes* (New York: Pergamon, 1973), 7.

6. John M. Good, *The Shaping of Western Society* (New York: Holt, Rinehart, and Winston, 1968), 19.

7. R.J. Shafer, ed., *A Guide to Historical Method* (Homewood, IL: Dorsey Press, 1974), 101.

8. Kay Stewart and Marian Freeman, *Essay Writing for Canadian Students* (Toronto: Prentice- Hall, 1981), 183.

9. Sheridan Baker, *The Practical Stylist,* 7th ed. (New York: Harper and Row, 1990), 43.

10. American Psychological Association, *Publication Manual,* 5th ed. (Washington, DC: American Psychological Association, 2001), 271.

11. William Messenger and Jan de Bruyn, *The Canadian Writer's Handbook,* 2nd ed. (Toronto: Prentice-Hall, 1986), 241.

12. Donald McCloskey, *The Writing of Economics* (New York: Macmillan, 1987), 4.

13. Sylvan Barnet, and Reid Gilbert, *A Short Guide to Writing about Literature* (New York: Addison-Wesley, 1997), 300.

14. William Zinsser, *On Writing Well,* 6th ed. (New York: HarperCollins, 1998), 39.

15. Joseph Gibaldi, ed., *MLA Handbook for Writers of Research Papers,* 5th ed. (New York: Modern Language Association, 1999), 117-18.

16. Edward de Bono, *Teach Your Child How to Think* (New York: Penguin, 1992), 10.

17. de Bono, *Teach Your Child,* 12.

Works Consulted

American Psychological Association. *Publication Manual*. 5th ed. Washington, DC: American Psychological Association, 2001.

Barnet, Sylvan and Reid Gilbert. *A Short Guide to Writing about Literature*. New York: Addison-Wesley, 1997.

The Chicago Manual of Style. 14th ed. Chicago: University of Chicago Press, 1993.

Crouse, Maurice. *Citing Electronic Information in History Papers*. 18 October 2002. <http://www.people.memphis.edu/~mcrouse/elcite.html> [5 January 2003].

de Bono, Edward. *CORT Thinking*. New York: Pergamon, 1973.

_____. *CORT 1: Teachers' Notes*. New York: Pergamon, 1973.

_____. *Teach Your Child How to Think*. New York: Penguin, 1992.

Gibaldi, Joseph, ed. *MLA Handbook for Writers of Research Papers*. 5th ed. New York: Modern Language Association, 1999.

Harnack, Andrew and Eugene Kleppinger. *Online! A Reference Guide to Using Internet Sources*. New York: St. Martin's, 2000.

Maggio, Rosalie. *The Non-Sexist Word Finder: A Dictionary of Gender-Free Usage*. Boston: Beacon Press, 1988.

Mann, Thomas. *The Oxford Guide to Library Research*. New York: Oxford University Press, 1998.

Payne, Lucile V. *The Lively Art of Writing*. Chicago: Follett, 1965.

Strunk, William and E.B. White. *The Elements of Style*. 4th ed. Boston: Allyn and Bacon, 2000.

Turabian, Kate L. *A Manual for Writers of Term Papers, Theses, and Dissertations*. 6th ed. Chicago: University of Chicago Press, 1996.

_____. *Student's Guide for Writing College Papers*. 3rd ed. Chicago: University of Chicago Press, 1976.

Zinsser, William. *On Writing Well*. 6th ed. New York: HarperCollins, 1998.